The
AFRICAN AMERICAN
EMPLOYMENT
GUIDE

Finding and Keeping a Job
Interviews — Networking— Career Goals

REFERENCE BOOKS

The
AFRICAN AMERICAN
EMPLOYMENT
GUIDE

Finding and Keeping a Job
Interviews — Networking— Career Goals

REFERENCE BOOKS

Compiled by
AMBER CLASSICS

Phoenix   New York
            Los Angeles

The African American EMPLOYMENT Guide

Compiled and Published by Amber Classics
An Imprint of Amber Communications Group, Inc.
1334 East Chandler Boulevard, Suite 5-D67
Phoenix, AZ 85048
Amberbk@aol.com / info@amberbooks.com
WWW.AMBERBOOKS.COM

Tony Rose, Publisher / Editorial Director
Yvonne Rose, Associate Publisher / Senior Editor
The Printed Page, Book Design

Rose, Tony, 1953-
  The African American employment guide : finding and keeping a job : interviews, networking, career goals / by Tony Rose.
      p. cm. — (Reference books)
  Includes bibliographical references and index.
  ISBN 978-1-937269-23-4 (alk. paper)
1. African Americans—Employment. 2. Minorities—Vocational guidance. 3. Job hunting. I. Title.
  HF5381.R757 2012
  650.14089'96073—dc23
                            2012006170

Contents

Preface

The African American Employment Guide is a Great and Dynamic Book!! Use this book to search for a job, change careers and negotiate promotions.

The African American Employment Guide avoids heavy analysis, but provides specific tips on each of the job seeker's major tasks, writing resumes and cover letters, filling out job applications, networking, and interviewing and backs them up with practical, easy-to-follow examples.

You, the Job Seeker, are encouraged to use this book as a guide, referring to various sections as the need arises.

Remember, however, that it is your effort, persistence, and follow-through, which will guarantee your ultimate success.

Chapter 1

Self-Assessment Profile

The self-assessment process involves an evaluation of your interests, abilities, and values. The first and foremost step is to find out about yourself and your desires. Think about what you would really like to do and accomplish in your career. What are the skills and capabilities you possess? A little thought along the way can pay high dividends in the end. After you have done some serious thinking, you will be better able to determine what type of employment you are seeking.

Next consider the environment that you would like to work in, such as the ethnic mix. Is it important to work for an Africa-American owned company, or are you comfortable in a more racially diverse business.

You should find a career that matches your interests, skills, and abilities by researching different career fields that coincide with your background. Some ways of doing this are by visiting the local library, the Internet, the college career planning and placement office, or the local employment office. Choose two or three areas of interest to start your job research project, but keep in mind that the job you seek now could be just the beginning of a series of career moves.

Career Goal-Setting

Knowing what career directions you would like to pursue is the first and foremost decision you need to make when beginning your job-search activities. By setting your career goals, you are able to work toward meeting specific objectives, measure your success, and achieve a feeling of self-gratification.

Being the Best You Can Be Means...
Taking Action!

Self-confidence comes when you are feeling good about yourself. This is an important quality which will make you more marketable in your search for a job.

If there are obvious racial undertones in the company you are pursuing, you may want to redirect your interests. After all, you will perform better and stand a better chance of advancing when you feel good about yourself.

Chapter 2

Types of Job Skills

Skills are special, and many job seekers think that they lack certain skills or that they have no skills because their definition of the word *skill* is not totally accurate. According to *Webster's Dictionary*, skill is defined as "practical ability and dexterity; knowledge, expertness, and aptitude."

A job seeker's skills can be identified in three ways. They are:

     1. Transfer skills

     2. Self-maintenance skills

     3. Job-related skills

Your job-search will be affected by the way you identify your skill groups and present them to a potential employer.

Transfer Skills

Transfer skills are those skills that are often referred to by employers as the "hire me" skills or the "universal" skill traits. These skills are transferable from one employer to the next and are commonly sought after by nearly all employers because they are so basic to job performance and success.

These skills are made up of skills that are gained from everyday living. Although you may fail to see that you possess them, these skills will assist you in meeting employers' expectations. Unlike the self-maintenance and job-related skills which are used in specific working conditions, transfer skills are used from one type of work to another without much effort on your part or much training from the employer.

The Transfer Skills Checklist on the following page will assist you in identifying the transferable skills that you have developed over the years. It is highly recommended that you take the time to follow the directions provided and do this exercise carefully. You should review the list several times because it will assist you in building your confidence and skills, which will increase your value to employers.

In addition to identifying your transfer skills, you will need to compile short statements to make about these skills in a job interview, so that you will be able to convince an employer that you are the best person for the job.

Transfer Skills Checklist

advise people	delegate
analyze data	deliver
anticipate problems	demonstrate
appraise service	design
arrange functions	detail
assemble products	detect
assess situations	determine
audit records	direct others
bargain/barter	dispense resources
be cost conscious	distribute
budget management	draft
buy products	earn quickly
buy services	edit
calculate numbers	encourage
chart information	endure long hours
check for accuracy	enforce
classify information	entertain
communicate	establish
compare data	estimate
compile statistics	evaluate
compute data	examine
conduct	exchange
confront others	exhibit
construct buildings	expand
consult with others	expedite
contact others	explain
control costs	explore
control situations	file records
converse with others	find information
coordinate activities	fix/repair
cope with deadlines	follow directions
copy information	gather materials
correspond	guide/lead
create	handle complaints

handle equipment	nurture
handle money	observe
help people	operate equipment
illustrate	organize data
imagine solutions	organize people
implement	organize tasks
improve	own a business
improvise	paint
inform	perceive needs
initiate actions	perform duties
inspect products	persuade others
instruct	plan
interpret data	policy-making
interview people	prepare materials
invent	produce
inventory	program
investigate	promote
lead people	protect property
lift (heavy)	question others
lift (moderate)	raise money
Listen	read references
locate resources	recommend
log information	record data
maintain	recruit people
manage a business	rectify
manage people	reduce costs
market materials	refer people
measure borders	rehabilitate
mediate problems	repair
meet the public	report
memorize info.	research
mentor others	resolve
monitor progress	retrieve
motivate others	review
negotiate	run meetings
Nurse	schedule

sell	tabulate
sequence	test
service	travel
set goals	troubleshoot
sew	type
signal	update
sketch	verify
socialize	visit
sort	volunteer
speak in public	weigh
study	write procedure
supervise	write proposals
supply survey	write reports
synthesize	write technical

Below are some examples which indicate how transfer skills can be used in a sample interview. Each is followed by an example that shows how it relates to a job.

Transfer skill statement: "I am always on time (prompt)."

Example: "While in school, I was never late."

Response: "If I was never late during school sessions and always met deadlines while in school, I will also be prompt and able to meet deadlines at work.

Transfer skill statement: "I keep good financial records."

Example: "As a homemaker, I handled all the family finances, which included the savings and checking accounts, and paid all the family bills on time, without any checks being returned for insufficient funds."

Response: "If I handled the family finances very well for thirty years, while taking care of other family responsibilities, I am sure that I can be a good and accurate bookkeeper for you."

Transfer Skill Statement: "I am a very organized person."

Example: "In my previous position, I had to organize my time and set priorities for seven bosses in order to get my job done to everyone's satisfaction."

Response: "If I could handle those complexities, I'm sure that I will be able to handle the organizational demands of this job."

Self-Maintenance Skills

Self-maintenance skills are sometimes called adaptive or personality skills. They assist the employer in identifying whether or not you, as a potential employee, have the temperament, finesse, or capability to adjust to the various demands presented by the job.

During the interview, the employer is trying to determine if you can handle the job or not, in terms of your ability to adapt to certain company demands or respond to certain people problems that may occur. Good workers can handle these problems while still doing quality work.

These self-maintenance skills are powerful and cannot be emphasized too much. Employers can always train people to do the work, but they cannot always train people to have enthusiasm for the work they are doing or like the people with whom they are working. Employers want people with good adaptive skills and a solid work ethic. Many employers would rather hire someone with less experience who can work well with others, than someone with more experience who cannot.

For the following exercise, select the self-maintenance skills that apply to you and write complete statements for each. Then include examples from your own experiences that support each statement. Finally, include a relationship between each skill and the job you want.

Self-Maintenance Skills Checklist

❏ accurate	❏ deliberate	❏ independent	❏ polite
❏ active	❏ democratic	❏ individualistic	❏ practical
❏ adaptable	❏ dependable	❏ industrious	❏ precise
❏ adventurous	❏ determined	❏ informal	❏ progressive
❏ affectionate	❏ dignified	❏ ingenious	❏ prudent
❏ aggressive	❏ discreet	❏ intellectual	❏ punctual
❏ alert	❏ eager	❏ intelligent	❏ productive
❏ ambitious	❏ easygoing	❏ inventive	❏ quick
❏ artistic	❏ efficient	❏ kind	❏ quiet
❏ assertive	❏ emotional	❏ leisurely	❏ rational
❏ attractive	❏ energetic	❏ likable	❏ realistic
❏ bold	❏ enterprising	❏ lighthearted	❏ reasonable
❏ broad-minded	❏ enthusiastic	❏ logical	❏ relaxed
❏ business-like	❏ firm	❏ loyal	❏ reserved
❏ calm	❏ fair-minded	❏ methodical	❏ resourceful
❏ careful	❏ farsighted	❏ meticulous	❏ self-confident
❏ cautious	❏ flexible	❏ mild	❏ sensible
❏ charming	❏ forceful	❏ moderate	❏ serious
❏ cheerful	❏ formal	❏ modest	❏ sensitive
❏ clear-thinking	❏ frank	❏ obliging	❏ sharp-witted
❏ clever	❏ friendly	❏ open-minded	❏ sincere
❏ competent	❏ generous	❏ opportunistic	❏ sociable
❏ confident	❏ gentle	❏ organized	❏ spontaneous
❏ conscientious	❏ good-natured	❏ original	❏ spunky
❏ conservative	❏ healthy	❏ outgoing	❏ stable
❏ considerate	❏ helpful	❏ painstaking	❏ steady
❏ cool	❏ honest	❏ patient	❏ strong-minded
❏ cooperative	❏ humorous	❏ persevering	❏ tactful
❏ courageous	❏ idealistic	❏ pleasant	❏ thorough
❏ creative	❏ imaginative	❏ poised	❏ tolerant
❏ tough	❏ unaffected	❏ versatile	❏ trustworthy
❏ thoughtful	❏ unassuming	❏ warm	❏ verbal
❏ trusting	❏ understanding	❏ wholesome	❏ witty

Self-Maintenance Skills Checklist

Statement:_____

_____

_____

Example:_____

_____

_____

Response:_____

_____

_____

_____

_____

Statement:_____

_____

_____

Example:_____

_____

_____

Response:_____

_____

_____

_____

_____

Job-Related Skills

Most people seeking work will know that the interviewer is going to ask them about their skills, but rarely are they aware of the need to present the employer with not only transfer skills and self-maintenance skills, but also a third group of skills: job-related skills. You must present and underscore the significance of all three skill traits to the employer's satisfaction.

Job-related skills are job-specific work skills. They include the vocabulary of the field that you are pursuing—the "buzz" words that relate to the job. For example, carpenters use levels, power saws, floor joists, etc. These words should be used in your interview to prove your knowledge or skill if you are applying for a carpentry job. On the other hand, if you are applying for a secretarial position, you would instead use words that identify what you would be doing as a secretary: for example, fax, hold, call waiting, ASAP, cc, Lotus, PowerPoint, etc.

Therefore, one can see that job-related skills could be considered "screening" skills for employers to determine who is the most qualified for the job by finding out who knows the language of the job better. These skills are actually learned by doing the work or by learning how to do the work while in school.

Job-Related Skills List

Specific job-related skills will include all the particular things that you can do or have done or will learn to do even better in the near future.

Listed below are examples of some simply-stated, specific skills:

- "I can type accurately."
- "I have 10 years of experience with child care administration."
- "I bus tables efficiently."
- "I have a talent for computerized cartoon sketches."
- "I relate well to people, both professionally and personally."

- ■ "I am experienced in all phases of household management."
- ■ "As a volunteer at the public library, I learned much about computerized retrieval systems."
- ■ "I can repair televisions, computers, and other digital equipment."

In the space below, list your special job-related skills.

Skills You Have

_____

_____

_____

_____

_____

_____

_____

_____

_____

_____

_____

Chapter 3

You and Your Resume

In preparation for a job-search, you will have to learn how to use various "paper tools." The resume is one of them. Don't hold back. List all your assets and get a professional opinion before you present your resume for a position. As an African-American, you should be prepared to know more than the job description calls for.

A resume will not guarantee you a job; it will, however, pave the way by drawing the attention of various employers to you. Your resume can tell prospective employers who you are, how to contact you, and what position you want. It will also describe your experience, skills, and abilities that are pertinent to the position you desire. A well-developed, organized, and neatly prepared resume will greatly improve your chances for an interview.

You may, perhaps, think that you do not need a resume. Depending on the job you want, this may or may not be true. However, many employers do expect resumes from their prospective employees. Your resume should satisfy the employer's expectations in the following ways:

■ Appearance
■ Content
  — Stability
  — Skill

Appearance

During interviews, many employers expect to see your resume, and if you have a neat and well-organized resume, you will have met an employer's initial expectation. Having your resume done professionally can be a worthwhile investment; and by all means use a good quality bond paper.

Content

This is what's in your resume.

Stability   Your resume will depict how stable you are to a potential employer by the pattern of your employment history. Omit short-term work history or combine several small, similar jobs into one entry. This illustrates a positive view of who you are and what you have to offer.

Skill   Your resume will demonstrate to the prospective employer how qualified you are. It does this by describing your skills, abilities, experience, and educational background. You may choose to enhance your resume more by emphasizing specific duties, accomplishments, and responsibilities from your work history. A highly rated resume would also define and quantify your skills in a way that would emphasize your worth as an employee.

The Chronological Resume

Resumes can be written in several different ways, but the most common ones are the chronological and the functional resumes. The chronological resume is traditionally used and usually lists, according to dates, your jobs and experiences in reverse chronological order; that is, usually the present or most recent experiences are listed first, then the next most recent, until the entire employment history is complete.

Refer to the examples on the following pages that illustrate how a chronological resume is organized. Take specific notice of how the items in the education and experience sections begin with the most recent information and work backwards from there.

The Functional Resume

The functional resume highlights your most important skills. It supports these skills with examples of how you have used them in the past. The functional resume emphasizes those skills that you believe are important to the position for which you are applying. To prepare a functional resume or any other type of resume, you must identify and highlight your skills. You must also know which of these skills will be required for the job you are seeking.

Before making a final draft of your resume, look over the following sample resumes for ideas regarding content and format. These examples illustrate how chronological and functional resumes should be presented to your prospective employers. They are from real people with differing backgrounds and objectives. Notice the individual differences that real resumes naturally show.

Chronological Resume

John Evans
36 Houston Road
Houston, Texas 39127
(555) 555-1212

Position Desired: Truck Driver

Summary of Work: Over 20 years of stable work history, including substantial experience with diesel engines, electrical systems, and all types of mechanical equipment. Good record-keeping skills and attention to details. Excellent driving record.

**Driving Record/
Licenses:**   Chauffeur's license, qualified and able to drive anything that rolls. No traffic citations for over 20 years. Accident-free record.

Vehicle Maintenance   Very careful in adhering to correct preventative maintenance schedules and avoid most breakdowns as a result. Substantial mechanical and electrical systems training and experience permits many breakdowns that do occur to be repaired immediately and avoid towing.

Record-Keeping: Excellent attention to detail. Familiar with recording procedures and submitting required records on a timely basis.

Routing: Knowledge of many states. Good map-reading and route-planning skills.

Other: Not afraid of hard work, flexible, get along well with others, meet deadlines, responsible.

Work Experience:

1993 – Present: Capital Truck Center, Houston Texas
Pick up and deliver all types of commercial vehicles from across the United States. Carry large sums of money and entrusted with handling complex truck-purchasing transactions.

1983 – 1993:	Blue Cross Manufacturing, Houston, Texas Received several increases in salary and responsibility before leaving for a more challenging position.
1977 – 1983:	Truck delivery of food products to destinations throughout the South. Supervised up to 12 men in the operations and maintenance of a variety of heavy equipment.
Prior to 1977:	Operated large diesel-powered electrical plants. Responsible for monitoring and maintenance on a rigid schedule. Conducted testing and inspection of electrical equipment.

Military

United States Air Force—Operated power plants, training in diesel engines and electrical systems. Stationed in Alaska, California, Wyoming, and other states. Honorable discharge.

Education

Cleveland Township High School, South Warren, Texas.

Personal

CB Radio Communications, Volunteer Fire Work, camping. Excellent health.

References available upon request.

Chronological Resume

Beverly Smith
75 Elmwood St.
Newton, IL 60617
(423) 763-1212 (Home)
(423) 590-1919 (Cell)

Position Desired

Seeking position requiring excellent management and secretarial skills in an office environment. Position could require a variety of tasks, including typing, word processing, accounting/bookkeeping functions, and customer contact.

Education and Training

Acme Business College, Indianapolis, IN

> Completed one-year program in Professional Secretarial and Office Management. Grades in top 30% of my class. Courses: word processing, accounting theory and systems, time management, and basic supervision.

John Adams High School, South Bend, IN

> Graduated with emphasis on business and secretarial courses. Won shorthand contest.

Other:

> Continuing education at my own expense (Business Communications, Customer Relations, Computer Applications, other courses).

Experience

1994 to 1997	Returned to Business School to update skills. Advanced coursework in accounting and office management. Learned to operate word processing equipment including Wang, IBM, DEC. Gained operating knowledge of computers.
1991 to 1994	Claims Processor, Blue Spear Insurance Company, Indianapolis, IN. Handled 50 complex medical insurance claims per day—18% above departmental average. Received two merit raises for performance.

1989 to 1991   Assistant Manager, Judy's Boutique, Indianap-
                          olis, IN. Managed sales, financial records,
                          inventory, purchasing, correspondence &
                          related tasks during owner's absence. Super-
                          vised four employees. Sales increased 15%
                          during my tenure.

1985 to 1989   Finance Specialist (E4), US Army. Responsible
                          for the systematic processing of 500 invoices
                          per day from commercial vendors.

                          Trained and supervised eight others. Devised
                          internal system, allowing 15% increase in
                          invoices processed with a decrease in
                          personnel.

1983 to 1985   Various part-time and summer jobs
                          throughout high school. Learned to deal with
                          customers, meet deadlines, and other skills.

Special Skills and Abilities
80 words per minute on electric typewriter, more on word proces-
sor, can operate most office equipment. Good math skills. Accept
supervision, able to supervise others. Excellent attendance record.

Personal
I have excellent references, learn quickly, and am willing to
relocate.

References available upon request.

Chronological Resume

Cecil R. Robbins
517 North Haines Street
Chattanooga, Tennessee 71317
(731) 456-1234 (Home)
(761) 456-2233 (Voice Mail)

Qualifications

Experienced in the use of most heavy-duty cleaning tools, such as wet and dry vacuum, buffer, and scrubber. Can use cleaning solvents and chemicals safely and properly to avoid both personal injury and damage to property.

Capable of performing several tasks in succession using personal judgment under minimal or no supervision. Instructed several employees in the correct working procedures and in setting proper standards for work quality. Experienced salesman capable of communicating well with public and representing company products.

Recognition

Received an award from employer for the cleanest, most respectable work area. Work was used to set the standard for other employees in their work performance.

Work Summary

1994 to Present   Holiday Inn, Chattanooga
Night janitor, promoted to day custodian. Supervise three janitorial staff, order supplies, schedule services for a busy 260-bed hotel with 12 meeting rooms and a restaurant facility.

1992 to 1994   Applegate Transit, Chattanooga
Janitor. Received two merit raises after accepting position. Loss of job due to a severe business downturn at Applegate.

Other

Get along well with others, efficient worker that gets things done, very reliable, have own transportation.

References

Available upon request.

Functional Resume

Todd M. Siegel
75 Curtis Lane
Tilton, NH 03276
(603) 555-6666

JOB OBJECTIVE: Day Care Center Assistant Manager

SKILLS

Curriculum Development: Planned curriculum units on Native American Studies, Forest Studies, and Dinosaurs for children aged 3-5 as part of practicum experience.

Wrote three children's books (unpublished) as part of Children's Literature course.

Art/Creativity: Planned, coordinated, and participated in creation of a full wall mural at Greater Vernon Boys' Club.

Experienced in introducing manipulative—paints, beads, and cooking to children aged 2-5.

Conferencing: Observed children in Kid's Inn Preschool Center and prepared weekly observation reports to be shared with classmates and site supervisor. Discussed feeding and toileting behaviors with parents of two young children under my supervision.

EDUCATION

Barlow Community College, Boynton, CO. A.S., Early Childhood Education, 1992. Course work included:

Creative Development   Exceptional and At-Risk Children
Day Care Organization   Children's Literature

Completed 120 hours of observation and 150 hours of practical training.

WORK HISTORY

Counselor, Greater Vernon Boys' Club, Vernon, CO, 2001-Present
Day Care Aide (practicum), Wunderkind Day Care, Clayton, CO, 2001
Deli Clerk, Ship 'N' Save, Vernon, CO, 2000
Child Care Provider, Ms. Mitzu Park, Vernon, CO,2000

RELATED INTERESTS

Big Brother, Big Brothers of America, Inc., 2000-Present

REFERENCES

Available upon request.

Functional Resume

Dana Brown
75 Curtis Lane
Tilton, NH 03276
(603) 555-6768

OBJECTIVE

Management trainee position in retail sales, using skills in design, administration, and public contact.

PROFESSIONAL EXPERIENCE AND SKILLS

Management   Coordinated operations, managed and assisted in sales at Peterson Stationery

Managed small medical laboratory at Petrie Laboratories.

Trained military personnel in Hazardous Waste procedures at Pease Air Force Base.

Administration   Wrote and catalogued procedures for medical laboratory in Bow, NH.

Designed new record forms, evaluated and carried out daily work priorities.

Coordinated numerous experiments from inception through subsequent interpretation and reporting of findings.

Special Skills   Type 75 wpm. IBM WordPerfect, Macintosh PageMaker.

WORK HISTORY

2001 – Present   Research Assistant—Petrie Laboratories, Bow, NH.

1999   Sales & Operations—Peterson Stationery, Concord, NH.

1996 – 1999   Hotline Volunteer—Women's Crisis Center, Generra, MA.

1985 – 1996   Family management and independent study.

EDUCATION

BS, Retailing, Metropolitan College for Women, Providence, RI.

References available upon request.

Functional Resume

LEE CUSIN
65 Clark Road
Tilton, NH 03276
(603) 555-6449

JOB OBJECTIVE

Bank Teller in a large metropolitan bank.

SKILLS AND EXPERIENCE

Customer Service
Handled customer inquiries and complaints at brokerage firm.

Educated and advised customers on new insurance products.

Sales
Solicited donations for renovations of community gardens.

Secretarial
Type 75 words per minute.

Experienced data entry clerk.

Recently completed coursework in Business Computer Applications.

EMPLOYMENT HISTORY

Insurance Agent	Whittemore Insurance, Natick,	2001-present
Office Assistant	Johnson Brokerage Firm, Stow,	1999-2001
Medical Assistant	Sam Donagan, MD, Gloucester,	1998-1999
Assistant Teacher	Wee Ones Day Care, Hyannis,	1997-1998

EDUCATION

A.S., Business Studies, Merritt College, Boston,	2001
Certificate & License, Medical Assisting, City College, Boston,	1996

References available upon request

Resume Outline

Resume Outline

Name: _____

Address: _____

Phone #: _____

Career Objective: _____

EXPERIENCE:

Company Name: _____ City/State: _____

Dates Employed: From _____ To _____

Position: _____

Responsibilities: _____

Company Name: _____ City/State: _____

Dates Employed: From _____ To _____

Position: _____

Responsibilities: _____

Company Name: _____ City/State: _____

Dates Employed: From _____ To _____

Position: _____

Responsibilities: _____

OTHER SKILLS: _____

_____

EDUCATION:

Year: _____ Name of School: _____

Course of Study _____

Degree: Yes _____ No _____ Type of Degree: _____

Year: _____ Name of School: _____

Course of Study _____

Degree: Yes _____ No _____ Type of Degree: _____

REFERENCES:

_____

26

Chapter 4

The Job Search Plan

Getting a job is hard work, but occasionally you may follow a lead right into a job. There are certain things, however, that must be taken into consideration. It is necessary to consider the differences between traditional and nontraditional job-hunting. Traditional methods refer to how things have always been done when seeking employment. Nontraditional job search methods, on the other hand, refer to steps and techniques that are out of the ordinary. Some of the traditional methods of looking for a job are:

- Going to personnel offices and filling out applications
- Reading the help-wanted ads in the newspaper
- Sending out resumes
- Going to the local government's employment service to wait in line and hope for a lead
- Going to job fairs
- Asking Friends and relatives
- Signing up with a private employment agency

All of these approaches have one common thread: they take a lot of time, and they keep you passive by forcing you to be indirect and dependent. You have to wait for someone else to do something for you. These traditional job search methods can foster a sense of helplessness, and eventually, hopelessness in the African-American community

The nontraditional job search method, on the other hand, uses unconventional ways of seeking employment, such as:

■ Looking at job listings furnished to community organizations such as Urban League and NAACP.

■ Seeking information from local planning boards regarding new businesses relocating and/or starting up in your community.

■ Seeking out a summer internship or volunteer work at a company to develop certain skills or enhance your reputation as a reliable employee.

■ Searching job search websites for categories that interest you.

■ Advertising your skills in the newspaper or on the Internet.

■ Networking with friends or relatives.

Seventy percent of all jobs are hidden and/or unadvertised. This, of course, is not to say that you should stop looking for jobs the traditional way, but rather that you should broaden your horizons in terms of job-hunting techniques.

While you will hear varied opinions regarding how to look for a job, most advisers seem unaware of how individuals really find jobs. Networking can play a very successful role in helping you learn about available jobs that are not advertised. For African-Americans who are making career moves, being referred by a long-time employee of the company you are pursuing has proven to be one of the best ways to get in.

A Job Search Plan is an organized plan of action designed for job seekers. There are certain procedures that you should develop in order to make your job search worthwhile. Begin with a time commitment. The time commitment refers to the number of hours that you will actually spend contacting employers, going to interviews, and doing tasks that support your efforts to talk to employers. The minimum recommended active job search time is twenty-five hours per week.

If you decide, for example, on forty hours, you have to keep in mind that this involves a highly structured job search week. It's not easy work, and you may wish to reduce the number of hours, but try to stick to your time commitment. Forty hours is not highly recommended because it is more than most people can do. A twenty- to thirty-hour job search schedule is more easily managed.

Your time commitment:

Write down the number of hours per week you plan to spend looking for a job:

_____hours per week.

Look at the following Sample Job Search Schedule, then complete your own job search schedule using the blank schedule that follows. Now that you have discovered how much time will be involved with your job search, it is important to decide how you are going to use that time. Remember, the primary objective is to get at least two interviews a day and to eventually become gainfully employed.

Sample Job Search Schedule					
Time	**Monday Activity**	**Tuesday Activity**	**Wednesday Activity**	**Thursday Activity**	**Friday Activity**
7:00-8:00					
8:00-9:00	Job Search	Job Search	Job Search	Job Search	Job Search
9:00-10:00	Job Search	Job Search	Job Search	Job Search	Job Search
10:00-11:00	Job Search	Job Search	Job Search	Job Search	
11:00-12:00	Job Search	Job Search	Job Search	Job Search	
12:00-1:00	Job Search				
1:00-2:00	Job Search		Job Search		
2:00-3:00	Job Search		Job Search		
3:00-4:00	Job Search		Job Search		
4:00-5:00	Job Search				
Evening	**Review and Plan for Tues.**	**Review and Plan for Weds.**	**Review and Plan for Thurs.**	**Review and Plan for Fri.**	**Review and Plan for Mon.**

Sample Job Search Schedule					
Time	**Monday Activity**	**Tuesday Activity**	**Wednesday Activity**	**Thursday Activity**	**Friday Activity**
7:00-8:00					
8:00-9:00					
9:00-10:00					
10:00-11:00					
11:00-12:00					
12:00-1:00					
1:00-2:00					
2:00-3:00					
3:00-4:00					
4:00-5:00					
Evening	**Review and Plan for Tues.**	**Review and Plan for Weds.**	**Review and Plan for Thurs.**	**Review and Plan for Fri.**	**Review and Plan for Mon.**

Results of Sending Unsolicited Resumes

By Type of Business	Invitation per Resumes Submitted	Interview per Invitations Received	Other per Interviews	Hire per Other
Aerospace	1:238	1:3	1:3	1:2
Business Machine/EDP	1:116	1:3	1:4	1:2
Petroleum	1:75	1:1	1:5	1:2
Communications	1:721	1:3	1:3	1:2
Electric/ Electronics	1:312	1:2	1:2	1:2
Chemical	1:126	1:2	1:2	1:2
Nuclear	1:36	1:3	1:2	1:3
R&D	1:85	1:2	1:3	1:2
Metal Working & Machinery	1:104	1:2	1:3	1:2
Others	1:1188	1:2	1:4	1:2
Totals (avg)	1:245	1:2	1:3	1:2

How Job Seekers Find Jobs: The Details

Method	Percentage of total job seekers using this method	Of all jobs obtained, percent obtained with this method
1. Applied directly to employer	66.0	34.9
2. Asked friends:		
about jobs where they work	50.8	20.2
about jobs elsewhere	41.8	10.5
3. Asked relatives:		
about jobs where they worked	28.4	6.1
about jobs elsewhere	27.3	2.2
4. Answered newspaper ads:		
local	45.9	12.2
non-local	11.7	1.3
5. Private employment agencies	21.0	5.6
6. State employment agencies	33.5	5.1
7. School placement offices	12.5	3.0
8. Civil service tests	15.3	2.1
9. Asked teachers or professors	10.4	1.4
10. Attended a job fair	1.4	0.1
11. Placed ads in newspapers:		
local	1.6	0.2
non-local	0.5	
12. Answered ads in professional or trade journals	4.9	0.4
13. Union hiring hall	6.0	1.5
14. Contacted local organization	5.6	0.8
15. Placed ads in professional or trade journals	0.6	
16. Other	11.8	5.2

How People Find Jobs

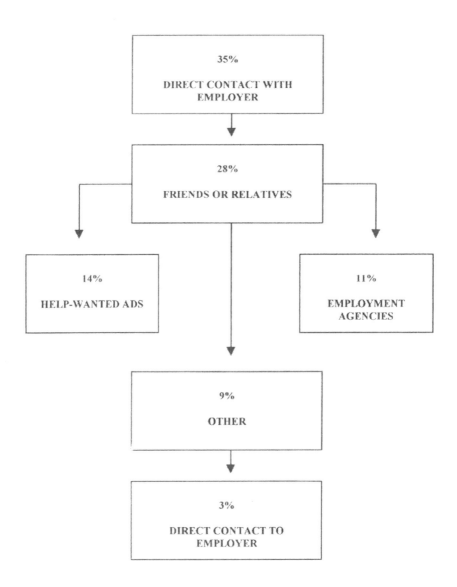

What is Networking?

Networking is a powerful tool to use when searching for a job. Many of the best jobs are not advertised; however, networking will help you find those job opportunities that seemed to be hidden. Networking is a process in which you contact people you know or people to whom you have been referred. You tell them what type of employment you are interested in and ask for their assistance in helping you find a job. They can help you in several ways: they might suggest a job opening that they know about, they might give you useful advice on where to search for a job, or they might give you useful advice about how to present yourself to a potential employer or identify those skills that might be most important to a potential employer. Most importantly, they can refer you to someone else they know who can help you in your job search.

Think about networking as something like a chain letter. You begin with people you know. Each person then refers you to someone they know, but you don't know. Your new contacts can then refer you to someone else they know, and so on. The potential is unlimited. You can literally develop a network of hundreds of people who are helping you with useful advice and who are "keeping their eyes open" for job opportunities that might come up in the future. Your church and social organizations are a good place to start.

The Rules of Networking

Step 1:   **Start Talking to Someone**

The basic criterion for networking with a person is that you have started a conversation with them. Relatives and friends are ideal places to start.

Step 2:   **Present Yourself in a Professional Way**

Whenever you present yourself to someone, it is important that they feel comfortable recommending you to an employer. It always helps to stay positive, friendly, well-organized, polite, and interested in what they say.

Step 3:   **Knowledge is Power**

If, in your conversation with your network contacts, you speak less than 75% of the time, you will probably learn something. But try to keep things centered on your goal: your job search.

Step 4:   **Get Referrals**

This is very important in developing your job network. Don't give up until you have at least two (or more) names of other people who might network with you in your search for a job.

Step 5:   **Referral Follow-Up**

Make an inquiry to your referral by calling him or her and saying, for example, "Hello, my name is Mary Jane. I'm a niece of Jack Bennett. He suggested that I call and ask you for advice. I am looking for a retail representative position, and he thought you would be willing to help me or give me a few ideas." The conversation will eventually take care of itself from there, but remember to keep it short on the phone. After the first few contacts with those people that you know, you will begin to quickly meet other people in your networking circle, because the nature of this networking process encourages each person to refer you to someone who knows even more or has more knowledge of the kind of job you want to do. The further you go into the process, the more people you see, the more you learn, and the better prepared you become. You are now operating in the hidden job market! Most people you meet this way may not have available jobs; however, they do know people that do, and will oftentimes tell you about them. This is the process of networking, and it really does help!

Step 6:   **Send a Thank-You Note**

A thank-you note is a simple act of kindness and appreciation that few people utilize. It is a form of social courtesy that demonstrates your ability to be considerate of others and that can leave a lasting impression upon your contact.

There are several important reasons for sending a thank-you note to those people who have helped you in your job search:

- They have spent valuable time with you in an interview.

- They have given you the name of a referral or referrals.

- They will remember you if something should come up in the future.

Whenever you conduct a job search activity, you should always do it on a person-to-person level. Thank-you notes will reinforce this one-to-one relationship. Thank-you notes are always advised because the people who receive them are far more likely to remember you. They will perceive you as being well-organized and thoughtful. Employers as a whole rarely received gestures of thanks from their prospective employees. They describe the people who do send thank-you notes as thoughtful, well-organized, and thorough. While a thank-you note may not get you the job you are seeking, it will help create a meaningful relationship with a person who will remember you. This common courtesy will ultimately make your new contact an effective member of your networking circle. If such a person as this knows of a job opening or meets someone who does, you will be remembered when others are not.

Tips for Preparing Thank-You Notes or Letters

1. **Paper and Envelope**

   Use premium quality paper with matching envelopes. Most stationery stores have this. Avoid "cutesy" covers. A simple "thank you" on the front will do. Buff or white colors are good.

2. **Typed Versus Handwritten**

   Handwritten notes are fine, but typewritten are better.

3. **Salutation**

   Unless you already know the person you are thanking, don't use his/her first name. For example, write, "Dear Mrs. Krenshaw" rather than "Dear Vera." Include the date.

4. **The Note**

   Always keep your note short and friendly. Never go into reasons for being hired. Remember, the note is a thank-you for what the person did, not a hard-sell pitch for what you want. As appropriate, be specific about when you will next be in contact. Even if you plan to meet with the person soon, send a note saying you look forward to meeting, and thank the person for the appointment.

5. **Your Signature**

   Use your first and last names. Avoid initials, and make your signature legible.

6. **When to Send It**

   Write and send your note no later than twenty-four hours after you make contact. Ideally, you should write it immediately after the contact while the details are fresh in your mind. Always send a note after an interview.

Following is an example of a thank-you note.

Sample Thank-You Note

August 20, 2011

Dear Mr. Smith,

Thank you for taking the time to talk with me this morning. As soon as possible, I will follow through with the names of the people you have given as referrals. I will call you again in two weeks, and let you know how it all works out.

Sincerely,

Tamika Ford

Basic Networking Techniques

Networking at the first level starts with your friend, Gail. She introduces you to two new contacts (the second level on your network), her friends, Donna and Bob, each of whom introduce you to at least two other people. This process can continue until your goals are achieved.

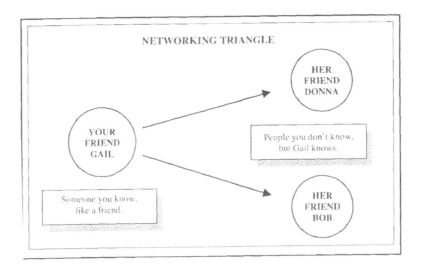

Below is a partial list of networking groups that have been used by job search workshops. You will probably use many of these and others of your own.

Sample Networking Groups

- Relatives, friends, former employers
- Co-workers, classmates from grade school/high school, etc.
- Current or former teachers and guidance counselors
- Members of your church, social club, athletic club, etc.
- People who sell things (at the store, insurance, etc.)
- People who provide you with services (hairdresser/barber, postal carrier, lawn service, etc.)
- People you play sports with and socialize with
- Neighbors
- Fraternity brothers/sorority sisters
- Members of a professional organization
- Parents of your children's friends
- Members of your political party

Job seekers often say that they "don't know anyone," and believe that most people get jobs because of who they know. While the latter part of this statement is true, keep in mind as well that you as a job seeker probably know more than enough people to secure the job you are seeking.

Make a separate list, using the form on the next page. Start with friends, then relatives, etc. Write as many friends' names as you can think of; then get their phone numbers. Complete the first two or three networking group lists, then save the other lists to do later in your job search. You may only need the first two.

My Networking Group

Name	Telephone Number
1.	
2.	
3.	
4.	
5.	
6.	
7.	
8.	
9.	
10.	
11.	
12.	
13.	
14.	
15.	
16.	
17.	
18.	
19.	
20.	

Keeping Referral Interviews on the Move

If you are shy and conversation does not come easily for you, here are a few questions you can ask in your networking referral interviews. These questions should keep the conversation going.

1. What inspired you to get into this line of work?

2. What are the things you like most (or least) about your work?

3. Do you have any ideas regarding how a person with my background and skills might find a job in this field?

4. What trends do you see in the career field? How could I take advantage of them?

5. What projects have you been working on that excite you?

6. From your point of view, what problems are most important to solve in this career area?

Cold Contacts

A cold contact is someone you have never met before. Many people need only use their warm contacts (someone they have met before) to develop a network that results in a job offer. It is wise, however, to use a variety of methods, including direct (cold) contacts with prospective employers. But you must remember that going from personnel office to personnel office requires time and gas. You may wish to initiate these cold contacts by a telephone call and a follow-up letter. The next page has an example of a cold contact follow-up letter that can oftentimes become rewarding for the job seeker.

Letter Following a "Cold Call"

August 16, 2011

Mr. Kelvin Lauder
Director
ABC Company
Lansing, MI 48164

Dear Mr. Lauder:

I appreciate your taking my phone call this morning. Our conversation increased my interest in ABC Company and confirmed my hope that my experience and skill could allow me to make a contribution there.

Enclosed is my resume for your consideration. Although most of my work experience has been in a manufacturing setting, I am certain that my ability to set goals and to lead and motivate diverse groups of people would successfully transfer to a company engaged in distribution.

The opportunity to meet you personally and explore future employment with ABC would be greatly appreciated. As you suggested, I will get in touch with you at the end of the week to see if a brief meeting can be arranged. If you have any questions or require further information, please feel free to contact me. Again, thank you for your time, and I look forward to our meeting.

Sincerely,

Barbara Johnson
Enclosure

To avoid making cold contacts in a haphazard manner, it is highly recommended that you take the time to develop general and specific prospecting lists such as those pictured below and on the next page. The time involved will be well spent. The use of such lists will help you identify a large number of potential employers in an organized and efficient manner.

General Prospecting List

Position/Job Desired ___ *Secretary*

#	Types of target organizations or businesses	Your level of interest (1=very; 2=somewhat; 3=not really, but possible)
1.	*Insurance Agencies*	1
2.	*Computer Companies*	3
3.	*Hospitals*	2
4.	*Advertising Agencies*	2
5.		

Begin by creating your own general prospecting form, using the same format illustrated in the sample. Fill in the type of job you are seeking. Then, on the numbered lines, list a few of the types of businesses or organizations that could possibly use a person with your skills. The obvious places will occur to you first. You should be able to think of at least three or four. Now, for each of these, think about how interested you are in working for that kind of business or organization. In the right-hand column, write the number "1," "2," or "3" to correspond with your level of interest.

Now that you have an idea of how the form works, turn to the Yellow Pages in the telephone directory. Find the index and begin with the first listing. For example, in the Atlanta directory, it is Advertising Agencies. For each listing in the index, ask yourself, "Could a person with my skills and experience work in this area?" If the answer is "yes" or "maybe," add that category to your General Prospecting List. Each time you add a category, give it the appropriate "1," "2," or "3." Let's say your job objective is "secretary" and you find Advertising Agencies in your directory. You may have answered "maybe" to the question of whether that kind of business could employ a person with your skills and experience. In that case, "advertising agencies" should be included in your list, with a "2" or "3" beside it. Even in large cities, if you spend an hour or so doing this, you can go through the entire Yellow Pages.

Next, look at the sample Specific Prospecting List below.

	Specific Prospecting List	
Position/Job Desired	*Secretary*	
#	Name of each specific organization to contact (from Yellow Pages)	Phone Number
1.	Acme Advertising	(614) 626-3341
2.	Abbotts Ads	(810) 223-4174
3.	Boyce Ad Agency	(248) 667-2134
4.	Catapal & Kline	(614) 336-7415
5.	Greg's Ad Agency	(614) 248-1671

Begin working on the Specific Prospecting List after you have completed your General Prospecting List. Each entry you have made on your General Prospecting List refers you to a section in the Yellow Pages, which, in turn, lists specific businesses and organizations to contact. List the names and telephone numbers of these businesses and organizations on your Specific Prospecting List. Each one of these individual listings is a potential target for you.

You now know far more than the average job seeker about finding job leads. Once you make meaningful contacts, it is important to stay in touch. Your contacts will hear of job openings that didn't exist when you last talked to them. In a very real sense, they will know of jobs opening up long before they are advertised. Since they already know you, staying in touch with them is often a far more effective source of good job leads than new contacts. Remember to send thank-you cards within twenty-four hours of your first contact.

Chapter 5

Job-Hunting Using the Internet

What You Need to Know about the Internet

When using the Internet for job-hunting, you will need to know how to navigate through the many job opportunities at a fast pace; otherwise, it will take many hours, and your job search might prove to be futile.

According to a survey by CDI Recruiters (NYSE:CDI), there are three important tips you must take into consideration when using the Internet during a job search:

1. Create a computer-friendly resume.

2. Know where and how to search.

3. Raise your profile on the Internet.

Create a Computer-Friendly Resume

Make it easy for your resume to be electronically transmitted and scanned into a database. Use a 10-point san serif typeface such as Helvetica, and avoid using bold, italicized, or underlined text, or lines or columns. Save your resume in ASCII text and basic Word versions.

Focus your online resume on the keywords you want to come up during a prospective employer's engine search. Online recruiters search for nouns or noun phrases that are descriptive of skills and capabilities, rather than the action verbs, which are commonly used on traditional resumes.

Avoid spelling and grammar errors—the basics still count. Have others take a look at your resume to help you eliminate errors. Update it frequently so that it comes up high on search engines.

Know Where and How to Search

Carefully research the various types of job sites. Which job sites are best for you? Job boards encompass several categories. Some are large, general-interest boards with thousands of jobs from all over the country. Other sites focus on jobs within a specific profession or industry. Regional sites focus on jobs in a particular geographic area. There are a growing number of job sites specifically associated with African-American and diversity related website.

Refine your search terms. Take time to review the help section of the job site you are using. Job sites use different search engines and understanding how the one you are using works will save you time.

Raise Your Profile on the Internet

Post your resume selectively. Use sites that specialize in your career area. Some sites allow you to block selected companies' access to your resume.

Participate in professional chat groups. Online chat groups and bulletin boards offer you a way to get noticed in an interactive environment.

The Internet Job Application

The electronic job application does not look like a conventional application for employment; instead, it only fills the purpose of a cover letter and resume. The fastest way to apply for a job on the Internet is to email your cover letter and resume to the desired person or organization. Your resume should be in plain text, ASCII, or DOS text if you send it via email. Include your cover letter in the same format as well, and make sure you mention in the letter where you found the ad for the job. Your resume and cover letter should be 65 columns (characters) wide because you want to make sure that your text fits the margins of different-sized monitor screens, otherwise it may wrap around and look bad. Your resume and cover letter should, of course, be sent together in the same file.

The Internet Resume

If you decide to post your resume on the Internet, here are some questions you might want to ask yourself:

- Do you want your resume information made public?
- Do you want it confidential?
- Can your resume be updated easily and at no cost?
- Will your resume be deleted if it is not maintained or updated periodically?

Do You Want Your Resume Information Made Public?
Once you post your resume on the Internet and into a database it will be considered a public document and out of your control. Even closed databases can be retrieved for public information. It is recommended that you post only your skills and a summation of your area of interest and expertise. Instead of providing a residence address on the resume, some people include only their email address and telephone number.

Do You Want it Confidential?
You can check the confidentiality of the database or service where you are placing your resume. This will determine who will be able to access your resume.

Can your resume be updated easily and at no cost?

Some services on the Internet will allow you to post your resume at no cost, but will charge you for updates. You don't want an old resume out there; nor do you want to post a resume where you will be charged to make an update. Ideally, you want to use services where you are able to update it an unlimited number of times at no charge.

Will Your Resume be Deleted if it is not Maintained or Updated Periodically?

Once you are gainfully employed, you don't necessarily want other employers calling you. Typically, a good job database will delete your resume after three months if it hasn't been updated.

The Great Galaxy of Job Listings

Listed below are several job-listing sites that will lead you through a galaxy of other job listings in your area of expertise.

Entry Level Job Sites

Entry-level job sites include summer employment, internship, and co-op job listings.

The College Career Consultant

www.careermosaic.com/cm/cc/
An excellent source for the college or high school student is the Career Mosaic Resource. After you review its list of employees, you can submit your resume directly to the Web site or you can link your resume with one of their internship sites.

The Career Hunter

www.interbiznet.com/hunt/
This Web site is linked to job listings of over 1,000 companies. The archives are available online along with other job resources.

The Black World Today/TBW Careers

www.tbwcareers.com
Your online source for job postings and free resume hosting. They act as career counselors to help you

define, locate, and successfully secure the right career opportunities.

The Princeton Review

www.review.com/careers/
The Birkman Career Style Summary is available for those job seekers who are unsure of the career choice that is right for them. You can also join the Career Discussion Group, search JobTrak for listings, or review Dilbert's Daily Mental Workout.

Student Center.Com

www.studentcenter.com/
This site is very helpful for the recent college graduate. Career advice and other planning tools are available.

The Youth Network of Canada

www.youth.gc.ca/

This site is created for youth in their preparation for the job hunt and workplace. It has partnerships with several agencies of the Canadian government and the Canadian private sector.

Co-ops, Summer Programs, Intercepts:

Career Center Internship Index

www.carleton.edu/cgi-bin/intern/internwais.pl
The student selects one out of twelve available categories and then searches for a position that is of interest. Ability to contact the business or organization directly.

Case Western Reserve University

www.cwru.edu/CWRU/Admin/cpp/summer.html
There are many summer jobs or part-time jobs listed at this site. These jobs are updated on a regular basis.

JobTrak

www.jobtrak.com
The college or university that you attend must be a member of JobTrak before you can gain access to it. You

can call your career center and ask for the password to access JobTrak. This site has an excellent reputation as a job seeker's resource.

Jobnet Internships

www.westga.edu/-coop/internships.html
At this site you will be linked to the Carter Center Internship program. It will provide you with several major companies and opportunities in many different disciplines.

Office for Special Learning Opportunities (OSLO)

oslo.umn.edu/
OSLO provides experiential learning opportunities for students at the University of Minnesota through its Internship Career Services, and Field Learning and Community Service program. It also provides students with other great internship opportunities nationwide.

University of California, Berkeley's Work Study Home Page

Workstudy.berkeley.edu/
The University of California Berkeley site is divided into an employer area and a student section with job search instructions. This is an excellent site for students that are looking for summer jobs and internship positions.

Government-Sponsored Opportunities:

AmeriCorps

www.cns.gov/americorps.html
AmeriCorps students do community service work for one year while earning money for college. Interested students should contact the National Civilian Community Corps or Volunteers in Service to America (VISTA) programs. Students can also consult the AmeriCorps Program Directory for a listing of hundreds of local community projects.

Project Vote Smart

www.vote-smart.org/

Students are selected through Project Vote Smart's National Internship Program. This project works with nonprofit organizations that research federal and state candidates and elected officials to provide information to the public regarding their voting records and positions on issues.

The White House Fellowships

whitehouse.gov/WH-Fellows/

The White House Fellowship Program provides gifted young Americans firsthand experience in the process of government, either in the Office of the President or in one of the Cabinet-level agencies.

Miscellaneous and Seasonal Work:

Summer Jobs

www.sumerjobs.com/

These summer jobs for students are linked to the *Wall Street Journal*'s top 10 job sites and other career training resources.

Teach for America

www.teachforamerica.org/

The National Teacher Corps sponsors recent graduates who are willing to commit two years of their lives to teach in rural and urban public school. Teacher certification is required.

Job Shadowing/Work-Study Programs

Listed below are three unique sites for college students that will allow them to experience the real world of work.

The Catapult, Career Service Professionals Home Page

www.jobweb.org/catapult/catapult.html

Jobweb, the National Association of Colleges and Employers

www.jobweb.org

America's Job Bank

www.ajb.dni.us

Researching the Business Organization of Potential Employers

Hoovers' Hotline
www.hoovers.com
Hoovers is a well-respected publisher of business almanacs. Its Web site provides information on over 10,000 companies.

Business Researcher's Interests
www.brint.com/interests.html
This is a source to research large businesses.

CompanyLink
www.fortune.com/lists/diversity/index.html
Lists the 50 best companies for minorities. They are committed to a multicultural workforce from the mailroom to the boardroom, and are doing what it takes to help minorities make the jump between the two.

Networking on the Net

Share some of your expertise with the online world and you'll receive great career opportunities in return.

If you want to make colleagues and industry "bigwigs" aware of you and your expertise, old-fashioned networking is a great method. By meeting and staying in touch with contacts via conferences, local meetings, phone calls, letters, email, and even Usenet newsgroups, you'll be remembered when interesting career opportunities arise or when you need help with a new business venture or job search. But since you probably network primarily with people in the same field or profession, attracting prospective clients or employers from unrelated areas can be a challenge. The key is to establish a presence that makes you known beyond your network and outside of place where you're usually found. Online it's called your "net presence."

Net Presence is defined as "the state or fact of playing a significant role in enhancing the Internet," (arganet.tenagra.com/Tenagra/net-presence.html). According to Tenagra, if you develop such a presence, good things will return to you.

Chapter 6

Telephone Communication Tools

There are many variations in telephone communication skills needed for a successful job search. However, there are four basic parts of a telephone contact that you should be familiar with:

1. The purpose of the call (which includes your full name)

2. The inquiry (the position)

3. What you have to offer (your skills and abilities)

4. The goal (an interview)

Effectively contacting employers can mean positive opportunities. But this is not easy for everyone to do because many people are simply afraid of being rejected or embarrassed. Simply ask yourself, "What is the worst thing that could happen?" (probably rejection for the job). On the positive side, using the telephone can be an effective job search technique. Only 25 percent of the available jobs are made public, and those are listed by local newspapers and federal and state employment agencies. The remaining 75 percent are considered the hidden job market. Since so few openings are actually made public, you can't wait to hear about those other possible job opportunities. You should always check the company in which you are interested to see whether or not they have job openings, because some openings may be hidden.

One way to contact those designated employers is to visit as many job sites as possible each day. However, this is not very efficient because you would simply be spending too much time and effort traveling and waiting to see people who are not expecting you. You would also find it very difficult to get past all of those receptionists who try to turn away job seekers.

A more efficient and cost-effective way of inquiring about possible employment is by using the telephone. Here are some of the advantages to using this approach:

- The telephone approach is cost-effective.

- Contacting employers can be done in just a few hours.

- The gathering of information can be easier and less time-consuming.

- You are more than likely going to talk to the person who is doing the hiring.

- Your chances of successfully preparing for an interview are greater because you will know what to expect.

The Purpose of the Call

(which includes your full name)

In any telephone conversation with the prospective employer, you should remember the two parts to the purpose of the call. First, you have to decide to whom you want to speak, either by name or position. Once you have reached the person, you need to say who you are and why you are calling. The surest approach is:

"Hello, my name is _____." Give your full name and do not say good morning or good afternoon—this opens up room for error because you may say "good morning" when it is, in fact, afternoon. Oops!

The Position

(the inquiry)

After your introduction, you need to immediately tell the employer what you want. Do not detain the employer or allow him/her to guess what you want. Instead, be specific, but tactful, in stating your desire for a job.

The recommended statement below is an example of how you can initially approach an employer in a tactful manner:

"I am interested in a position as a _____."

The word "position" is used as opposed to the word "job." This is tactfully saying what you want. Most employers frown on the word "job" because they feel that the applicant is only interested in obtaining the position for monetary purposes. They want to know that the applicant is also interested in a career. When using the telephone to inquire about employment, try to avoid using such statements as:

- I'm calling about the job you have listed.
- Do you have any jobs available?
- My skills are
- Do you have a job for me?

Your Skills and Abilities

(your qualifications)

This is the most important part of the telephone contact because it briefly identifies yours skills and abilities. This is what may intrigue the employer and make him/her want to listen to you more. This conversation by itself will ultimately set you apart from all other applicants because most applicants will just ask for "any job" and mention no qualifications. Your qualifications show action and tell the employer what you have done.

An Interview

(the goal)

The primary purpose of the telephone contact is to obtain an interview. How you state your goal will depend on whether or not you know the person you are calling, and whether you have been referred by someone or have simply found this person's name in the phone book. Getting an interview will always be the main goal of your phone contact, but there are actually three additional goals: referrals, information, and help, which are important if your primary goal is not achieved.

First Goal: An Interview
Always ask three times if necessary! (1) If no jobs are open now, ask to interview for future ones. (2) If the person is too busy to see you, offer to meet the following week, or as soon as convenient. (3) If the person is unwilling to set up an appointment now, ask if it is okay to check back; then set a date and time to check back. Be sure to call back as promised!

Second Goal: A Referral
If you can't get an interview, try to get a referral. Ask if the individual knows anyone else, either in that same organization or in any other organization, who might use someone with your skills.

Third Goal: Information
If you can't get an interview or a referral, try to get useful information about the individual's organization or similar organizations that might fit your employment prospects, or ask how you might improve your presentation.

Fourth Goal: Help
Get more help from your contact later. You can ask for a critique, such as "Do I seem to be the kind of person who would fit into this field if you were hiring?" You can also ask, "Can I call back for more help later if I need it?"

Your Telephone Contact

The following page shows samples of telephone contact sheets. You may write out your own as well, but you may have to write it out several times before it makes any sense to you. Keep making changes until it sounds just right for you.

Telephone Communication Sample Form

Telephone Communication Sample Form		
(Answering Help-Wanted Ads)	**Date:**	7/12/11
Company Name and Address	**Person to Contact (Full Name & Title**	**Telephone Number**
Accron Corporation	Keith Lauderdale	(313) 456-7128
1616 Industrial Hwy.	Personnel Director	

Call Objective: (Check One)
☑ Help-Wanted Ad   ☑ Referral
☑ Appointment   ☐ Other
☐ Information

Referral From:

Relationship to Referred Person:

Introduction: Hello, my name is Darryl Williams. I am calling in regards to your ad in the newspaper for a janitorial position. May I speak to the person in charge of interviewing for this position?

Outline of Script: Hello, Mr./Mrs._____, my name is Darryl Williams, and I am inquiring about the janitorial position you have advertised in the newspaper. I have janitorial experience in warehouse and manufacturing, and I think you'll find me as a flexible and excellent employee. May I come in today or tomorrow for an interview?

Conclusion: Ask yourself these questions before concluding the telephone call:

	Yes	No	Comments
Did I accomplish my call objective?	☑	☐	
Did I get an interview?	☑	☐	
Did I get a referral?	☐	☑	
Did I get information?	☑	☐	
Did I get help?	☐	☑	
Other Comments?			

Follow-Up Action to be Taken:

Names of Referrals

Interview date: _____ 7/19/11 _____   Sherry Johnson

Referrals follow-up date: __7/16/11__

Send resume: _____ 7/13/11 _____

Fill out application: _____7/19/11_____

Other: _____

If you have trouble perfecting your phone contact, ask your instructor or a friend for help. Rehearse your presentation with friends and family. The more you say it aloud, the more natural it will sound and feel to you. Often when you are inquiring about a position with a company, you may talk with secretaries or receptionists. Their job, among other things, is to screen phone calls for their boss. They may seem suspicious, but you should not be discouraged because this is a common business practice. It has been proven that if you treat them well over the telephone, they can help you in your job search. However, if you do not treat them well or with respect, it has been proven that your chances of getting a job with that particular employer will be very difficult. Describe to the secretary or receptionist the type of position you are seeking and ask what you might do to be considered. You never know; a positive comment from the secretary may be worth as much as a good resume. The good news is that in many companies, the front office person is usually African-American.

On the following page are examples of telephone etiquette techniques that you should take into consideration when using the telephone to contact prospective employers.

Examples of Telephone Etiquette

How to Communicate Effectively with the Receptionist on the Telephone	How to Communicate Effectively with the Secretary on the Telephone
■ Do not identify yourself to the receptionist unless asked to do so. ■ Always be polite and courteous. ■ Remember, the receptionist's job is to route phone calls to the correct party. ■ Ask if there is a direct-dial number for the person you are calling, once identified. ■ Job titles vary by company and industry. When dealing with the receptionist (first person answering the phone), don't be surprised if she replies: "We have no on here by that title." Be prepared to offer further clarification describing the function of the individual to whom you wish to speak. ■ Always begin your conversation by saying: "Can you tell me the name of the..." (the person who has the authority to grant you an interview). ■ Once the person has been identified, immediately ask to speak to him or her. ■ If calling long distance, always begin your inquiry by saying: "I'm calling long distance."	■ When the secretary answers the phone, immediately identify yourself, for example: *This is Mr. (Ms.) from Combacker Corp. in Madison, WI. Is Mr. Thomas in?* ■ If not in, ask when it would be convenient for you to return the call. ■ Try calling back at least once, if possible. ■ Never refuse a secretary's offer to help you. ■ When accepting her offer of help, first find out the secretary's name and position, courteously. Write this information down. ■ If the secretary suggests your inquiry be routed to personnel, you can use the following responses: *I'd be happy to contact personnel. Who should I ask for?* Then, *"I just spoke to _____ office and they suggested that I speak directly to _____ about possible future openings in his/her department."* ■ In future calls, always use the secretary's name.

Chapter 7

Your Cover Letter

Unless you are personally handing a resume to a prospective employer, you should prepare a cover letter or letter of application, and mail it with your resume. Your cover letter gives you the opportunity to state which position you are applying for and why. It will also emphasize your strong points and give you the opportunity to ask for an interview.

Cover letters should always be addressed to a specific person whenever possible. The cover letter should be addressed to that individual who would potentially be your supervisor, not to the human resources department.

There are variations in the standard cover letter approach. These variations depend mostly on the circumstances of the desired position. However, virtually every standard cover letter follows these guidelines:

1. Present your cover letter on good quality stationery with matching envelopes, preferably the standard 8½ x 11 paper size, usually white or ivory-colored.

2. Use computer-printed cover letters to present a professional appearance.

3. Use appropriate standard business formats (see examples for standard business-correspondence formats on the following pages).

4. Always begin your correspondence by mentioning prior contacts, if any; provide a friendly review/reminder of these prior contacts and the reason for your correspondence.

5. Remember to research the organization so that you can discuss professionally in your cover letter your skills and experiences and how they relate to that particular position.

6. Close your letter by requesting an opportunity to have an interview.

The following pages provide a cover letter format and sample cover letters for designated business contacts.

The Cover Letter Format

1. HEADING   →   Today's Date

2. INSIDE
   ADDRESS   →   Employer's Name
   Employer's Address

3. SALUTATION   →   Dear Mr. _____

I am interested in _____
_____
_____

4. BODY OF
   LETTER   →   Recently I worked at _____
_____
_____

I will be available _____
_____
_____

5. CLOSING   →   Sincerely Yours,

6. SIGNATURE   →   Your Signature
   Your Name (typed)

Your Name
Your Address   STAMP

Employer's Name
Employer's Address

Direct Approach

September 15, 2011

Mr. Tom Smith
Manager
Manufacturing Consultants
Cincinnati, OH 40340

Dear Mr. Smith:

The plant where I have been employed as a General Sales Manager for the past 12 years will be closing this month. I am very interested in being considered for a position in your plant in Sales, Marketing, or in any capacity where my skills could be used. I am very familiar with all phases of the manufacturing of truck parts.

Enclosed is my resume for your review. My qualifications also include an outstanding sales record and commendations by supervisors for the quality of my work and my ability to motivate others.

I have over 20 years of management experience in the manufacturing arena and look forward to an opportunity to use my knowledge in a new setting. I would like to meet with you briefly, to discuss career opportunities at Manufacturing Consultants. I will call next week to see if your schedule permits such a meeting. Thank you for your consideration.

Sincerely,

Jean Howard

Enclosure

Response To Ad

November 17, 2011

Ms. Margaret Bailey
Manager
National Tech Team
Columbus, OH 46714

Dear Ms. Bailey:

I am applying for the position of Executive Secretary in response to the advertisement in the Columbus Star, November 15, 2002.

My qualifications, as detailed in my enclosed resume, match the described position very well. I have functioned both as an executive secretary and an administrative assistant, reporting directly to a plant manager and several vice presidents in the automotive manufacturing environment. I type 75 wpm with 100 percent accuracy, have experience with WordPerfect, Lotus 1-2-3, and Power Point, and am proficient in using shorthand. Supervising and organizing a well-run office are my strengths. My former supervisors will attest that I enjoy a busy work environment and love the challenge of learning new things.

I am available for an interview at your convenience and would enjoy the opportunity to discuss this position and my qualifications in more detail. I look forward to hearing from you.

Sincerely,

Denise Jones

Enclosure

Networking Letter

December 20, 2011

Ms. Ann Stubblefield
Ameritech
2722 Michigan Ave.
Detroit, MI 48203

Dear Ms. Stubblefield:

I am contacting several friends to ask for assistance and advice. You may have heard about the merger here at XYZ Company. We've been bought out by Comco, Inc., and our facility will close at the end of July. As a result, I find myself reentering the job market.

After a lot of self-assessment and reviewing of my career goals, I've decided to seek a managerial position in the accounting/financial/MIS field. I would prefer a company that is growing and expanding, but I am open to almost any good opportunity in any industry.

I know that the positions I am looking for usually do not appear in the classified ads, so I am hopeful that you might be able to refer me to a friend, an acquaintance, a business associate, or (ideally) an individual in a company who would be interested in my capabilities. The enclosed resume will bring you up to date on my career and give you a good idea of the qualifications that I possess.

I appreciate your interest and look forward to talking with you in the near future.

Regards,

Nelson Powell

Enclosure

Thank-You for Referral

February 22, 2011

Ms. Gail Moore
3642 Palomino Drive
Los Angeles, CA 06477

Dear Ms. Moore:

Thank you for referring me to Sam Harrison at Pioneer, Inc. We had a very interesting discussion over the telephone, and he asked me to forward my resume. Although he has no openings at this time, he was very enthusiastic about my qualifications. I emphasized the work I did at Telecom, as you suggested, and that proved very helpful. He suggested I stay in touch with him as his company is approving new budgets in the next few weeks.

I'm still trying to set up a meeting with Herb Scott, but he's been out of town. His secretary remembered you, however, and I think that will help me to get an appointment.

Again, thank you. I will continue to keep you posted on my progress. With your assistance and support, this job search is bound to be a success.

Regards,

Joyce Wells

Job Announcement/Referral

January 10, 2012

Mr. Wally Cunningham
General Manager
XYZ Company
Terre Haute, IN 66741

Dear Mr. Cunningham:

Happy New Year!!! Thank you for your referral and kind advice, I am pleased to announce my new position with XYZ Company. I can't tell you how much your support has meant to me. A job search can be a lonely endeavor if one doesn't have a solid network of friends like you. I'm truly grateful.

Now that I'm re-employed, we'll have to have lunch. I'll be calling you soon. Again, thanks, and if I can ever be of any assistance to you, please let me know.

Best regards,

Donnell Edwards

Informal Interview

August 14, 2011

Mr. Mike Marjoram
Tech Mate Corp.
5326 Willow Lane
Chicago, Illinois 37864

Dear Mr. Marjoram:

I sincerely enjoyed our meeting today, and wish to thank you for your insights and the information you provided about opportunities at Tech Mate Corp. The tour was fascinating, and your staff impressed me with their enthusiasm and openness.

After reviewing our discussion, I am convinced that there is a solid match between my expertise and your requirements. The position you described would indeed be the challenge I've been seeking. I'd like to propose a follow-up to our meeting. After today, I know that the demands on your time are very great, so I will make myself available at your convenience.

Again, thanks for your time, and I'll look forward to hearing from you in the near future.

Sincerely,

Joann Gibson

Helpful Cover Letter Hints

Some helpful hints in mailing out cover letters are:

1. Monday is considered a heavy mail day, so you will want to post your letters to arrive on Tuesdays or later in the week. They will get more attention.

2. Try to call within two days of the company's receipt of your letter to arrange for an interview.

3. Because Monday tends to be hectic, You will have better luck if you try for interviews later in the week.

Chapter 8

Dress For Success

As you enter the office where the interview will be held, the employer will immediately notice how you have dressed for the interview.

People form an opinion within the first five seconds of interview/employer contact. That is why it is so important to come prepared for your interview.

There are four factors of appearance that are important to employers:

1. How you look
2. How you act
3. How you write
4. How you speak

How You Look

There are three aspects of the how you look which also reflect your appearance: how you dress, how well you are groomed, and your personal hygiene.

The Way You Dress

There are some basic rules you should follow when dressing for an interview:

1. Always dress one step above what you would actually wear on the job. For example, if on the job you would wear a casual skirt and blouse or casual shirt and pants, you should wear a dark-colored conservative suit to the interview. You can also find out what the company employees are wearing by visiting the company before the interview. Or, take notice of the dress of other employees with jobs quite similar to the one you are seeking. After a few interviews, you will become well acquainted with how to adjust your dress to fit the situation.

2. Never wear informal clothing such as T-shirts, jeans, or tennis shoes to an interview.

3. Don't wear ethnic clothing unless you are part of a strict religious group with a mandatory dress code. (In this case, your potential employer must be made aware of your specific religious needs before they hire you.)

4. Always wear clothing that is clean, neat, and in good condition. Buy quality and well-fitted clothing and use it only for interviews.

5. The dress theme for an interview is to always dress conservatively! Never wear loud colors or prints. Avoid mismatched colors and patterns, such as pink with orange or plaids with stripes. The price to pay for wearing the "fad" style is unemployment. List some of the ways you would dress for an interview, and then compare them to the examples listed above.

6. Women should avoid wearing "high" heels (a medium or low pump works well) and always wear stockings. Men should wear a polished plain shoe (never sneakers). Work boots only work for heavy labor positions.

7. Short, tight, and low-cut are big No's for women. Baggy and droopy wear are major turnoffs for men.

My Dress for success plan of action is:

1.	6.
2.	7.
3.	8.
4.	9.
5.	10.

8. Give yourself a dress rehearsal before the interview. Take time to dress exactly as you would for your interview and then ask a friend or relative for comments. Rehearse in front of a mirror if there is no one to give helpful comments.

How Well Are You Groomed?

Grooming, of course, plays an important role in our appearance. Listed below are some basic "rules of thumb" that define what good grooming is.

1. Well-groomed hair should always be clean, combed, and neatly styled. (Avoid trendy or fad styles. Stay away from braids that may be overstated; bright colors and bouffant). Do a little research and find out what is "acceptable" in the particular workplace you are aspiring for.

2. Men should always shave before an interview, and if they wear mustaches or beards, they should be neatly combed and trimmed. Mustaches and beards in their early stages do not look presentable.

3. Long fingernails should be trimmed. Women should wear only natural colors (avoid bright and dark shades).

4. Makeup and perfume should be used sparingly.

5. Be sure to use lotion on ashy hands, elbows and knees.

List some of the ways you would groom yourself ahead of time for an interview, and then compare them to the examples listed above.

My Grooming Plan of Action is

1.	6.
2.	7.
3.	8.
4.	9.
5.	10.

Your Personal Hygiene

Grooming, hygiene, and dressing for success are all closely related. But if you neglect one, you will hurt the others. If, for example, you are well dressed and well groomed, your personal appearance will falter if you overlook your hygiene.

Listed below are some positives regarding your personal appearance and hygiene.

1. Always keep your body clean. Good personal hygiene begins with a clean body.

2. Wash your hair on a regular basis.

3. Brush and floss your teeth daily.

4. Use deodorant.

5. Always have clean fingernails.

*Remember—44 percent of the people who stay unemployed do so, in part, because their personal appearance does not reflect the employer's expectations.

How You Act

Manners are another part of appearance that employers take into consideration. The word *manner* refers to your personal behavior. How you behave in an interview reflects how you might behave on the job. Since you have limited time to give a positive impression to an employer, make sure that your manners are intact.

During your interview, your manners should be natural and positive. You will make a good impression if you conduct yourself with confidence and common courtesy. Do not, however, overreact. Let your honesty and sincerity stand out in a confident and courteous way.

How You Write

Your appearance also involves how your paperwork materials, such as your application, look when completed. Your paperwork must be filled out in a way that shows the employer that you are neat, complete, and accurate.

How You Speak

Your manner of speaking is of the utmost importance during the interview and even during your telephone phone contacts. Good communication skills mean doing the following:

1. Organize your thoughts before speaking.

2. Speak with enthusiasm and confidence.

3. Talk to the employer about achievements and the results of those achievements and how you can help the employer.

4. Use proper names and clear diction.

5. Never use slang or ebonics and stay away from making jokes.

Employers like to hire people who portray good verbal communication skills. Be one of the skilled communicators.

Chapter 9

Stress Management

We all feel a certain amount of stress in our lives on a daily basis. There are two types of changes in life that pose stress. One is slow and gradual, and the other happens all at once. The latter is usually a major change.

An example of the first type of stress is when you changed grades in school. You were familiar with the school, the teachers, and the classroom. You knew basically what to expect, even when you changed grades. This was a gradual change; it was not too stressful.

An example of the second type of stress is your first day at a new school where you didn't know anyone, not even the teachers. In such a case, you would be unfamiliar with the school grounds and would have no one in particular to ask for help. You might even be the only African-American student or one of a few. You would probably feel lonely and awkward. That would be a sudden, major, stressful change.

Stressful Situations

We all will experience a certain amount of stress as we encounter:

1. Job-hunting and interviewing
2. New-job adjustment
3. New supervisors
4. Day care and transportation problems
5. Getting along with new co-workers
6. Fitting in at a company that is not well-integrated

Typical Reactions to Stress

Some typical reactions to stressful situations are:

1. Heart palpitations
2. Headaches
3. Sweaty palms
4. Nervousness
5. Nightmares
6. Insomnia
7. Upset stomach
8. Dry mouth

You'll probably experience one or more of these when you start your new job. It's normal. Usually the stress is worse when you're closest to the change.

There are at least 16 ways to reduce stress:

1. *Listen to Music.* Psychologically, music helps a person to relax, enjoy pleasant memories, or stimulate positive emotions.

2. *Do Aerobics.* Fitness experts claim that aerobic exercise (running, skating, cycling, swimming) can ease anxiety and muscle tension, reduce depression, and help you stay low-key under pressure

3. *Eat a Nutrient-Dense Diet.* You can't avoid stress, so you might as well arm yourself nutritionally against attacks. That means build up a stress-fighting reserve with nutrients that are often depleted by stress: vitamins B and C, potassium, magnesium and zinc, which are necessary for maintaining a

healthy nervous system. A bonus tip: take a multivita-min/mineral supplement.

4. *Hug Your Pet.* Animals can have a big impact on physical and mental health. Caring for a pet can help lower blood pressure and reduce stress. Plus, pets provide their owners with a sense of security. "Pets don't make demands of us, so we're getting an unconditional show of affection, acknowledgment and warmth.

5. *Take a Bath.* Hydrotherapy has been used for centuries to induce relaxation. Many medical experts know firsthand that warm water can be soothing. To relax, I take hot baths teamed with aromatherapy and I use essential oils.

6. *Wash Your Hands.* Hand washing is a quick and easy stress reliever that you can do almost anywhere: at work, home or even a party.

7. *Organize Your Space.* Clutter can be a big source of stress. Organize a closet or drawer one by one; toss out things you don't use, recycle newspapers and magazines, and toss out junk mail.

8. *Read a Book.* According to medical experts, reading is a great natural sedative. It's a readily available indulgence that provides an inexpensive escape. It's good to give yourself time out, and then come back and look at a problem you may be having.

9. *Eat Less Stress-Causing Food.* Want to minimize stress? A good place to start is by eliminating all food fare that may frazzle nerves. Some common diet culprits are coffee, tea, sodas, sugar, and chocolate. Stress-fighting nutrients needed to cope with stress are depleted by too much sugar and coffee.

10. *Learn to Smile and Say "No."* Want a surefire tip on how to troubleshoot stress? Think before saying "yes" to an extra project, social event, or "quick" errand. Chances are it will eliminate unnecessary frustration and turmoil.

11. *Take a Deep Breath.* You can control stress by focusing on breathing. Consciously slow your breathing down, think of exhaling out your problems and tensions you feel. Visualize

new energy entering your body. By slowing and deepening your breathing you'll be in a more relaxed state as your body influences your mind to calm down.

12. *Talk to a Friend.* Feeling troubled? Pick up the phone and reach out to someone you know. Or better yet, make a social call. Chatting and renewing friendships can strengthen bonds and calm both parties.

13. *Take a Hike.* Taking yourself away from an indoor environment and going outdoors can help to de-stress the body, mind, and spirit. Hiking through a natural, scenic park can relax and recharge your body. A 30-minute hike not only beats stress, but it also burns calories and speeds up your metabolism, which can help keep you fit and trim.

14. *Think Before You React.* Before reacting to a high-stress situation, try to understand it first. Counting to ten before you react can enable you to respond more effectively. Look at what's being said by thinking first, before you react. This way, you can take things seriously instead of personally.

15. *Take Care of Yourself.* Inevitably, when you get stressed, it's easy to forget to take care of yourself. Many people fall victim to busy schedules by not eating the right foods, losing sleep, and using unhealthy stress reducers.

16. *The Basics.* Eating right, getting adequate sleep, avoiding alcohol and cigarettes, and exercising are keys to getting your body strong and ready to fight stress-related diseases.

17. *Go to the Movies.* Spending time away from work or home can often be key components to changing your stress level. Seeing a movie is a temporary fix, but a refreshing change.

18. *Take a Weekend Retreat.* A short drive to a nearby resort can work wonders. Go somewhere with a spiritual essence or a physical component such as horseback riding.

19. *Dance.* What a workout this can be. Take your favorite dance partner or go somewhere that you can meet new partners. The "electric slide" works wonders and you don't even need a partner. Or, if you take dance class you'll gain routine to look forward to.

How Vulnerable Are You to Dangerous Stress?

Score each item from 1 (almost always) to 5 (never), according to how much of the time each statement applies to you.

____ 1. I eat at least one hot, balanced meal a day.

____ 2. I get seven to eight hours sleep at least four nights a week.

____ 3. I give and receive affection regularly.

____ 4. I have at least one relative within 50 miles on whom I can rely.

____ 5. I exercise to the point of perspiration at least twice a week.

____ 6. I smoke less than half a pack of cigarettes a day.

____ 7. I take fewer than five alcoholic drinks a week.

____ 8. I am the appropriate weight for my height.

____ 9. I have an income adequate to meet basic expenses.

____ 10. I get strength from my religious beliefs.

____ 11. I regularly attend club or social activities.

____ 12. I have a network of friends and acquaintances.

____ 13. I have one or more friends to confide in about personal matters.

____ 14. I am in good health (including, eyesight, hearing, teeth).

____ 15. I am able to speak openly about my feelings when angry or worried.

____ 16. I have regular conversations with the people I live with about domestic problems, (e.g., chores, money and daily living issues).

____ 17. I do something for fun at least once a week.

____ 18. I am able to organize my time effectively.

____ 19. I drink fewer than three cups of coffee (or tea or cola drinks) a day.

____ 20. I take quiet time for myself during the day.

____ TOTAL

Chapter 10

The Job Application

The job application is an employment tool that most job seekers are familiar with. It also contains pertinent questions about a job seeker's personal and work-related experience.

The Application:

1. Collects employment data about you.

2. Indicates the job location you desire.

3. Allows personnel to screen out those applicants that appear undesirable, by eventually highlighting an applicant's weaknesses.

In some instances, the job application is just as critical to the employment screening process as the resume. A resume, however, can never be substituted for an application for employment.

Filling Out the Application

If you feel too limited by the space provided on an application, attach additional sheets or your resume. Unlike the resume, an application for employment demands responses to very specific questions. Of particular concern to employers is your education, experience, and other relevant activities which describe how your time has been spent for the past several years.

If there are gaps in your working life, be prepared to explain them. Fill out an application completely. If information is requested that you choose not to provide, indicate this in some way—either with an explanation or by drawing a line through the response box, or, if appropriate, by putting N/A (not applicable) in the space provided, but be judicious about this. Clearly an employer is interested in, and has a right to know about, your education and work experience. You must accurately complete all of the questions on the application. You may be asked and should expect to provide your:

1. job titles, names of supervisors, and dates of employment,

2. salary or wages from previous employment, and salary or wage expectations, and

3. reasons for leaving other jobs (see the next page).

State all information in a positive manner. Negative information will hinder you. Be particularly careful about reasons for leaving. You are *not*, however, required to furnish information about your:

- Age
- Sex
- General state of health
- Religion
- Marital status
- National origin

The following page lists some positive reasons for leaving a job. Can you think of some for your application for employment?

Positive Reasons for Leaving A Job

1. I desired a more challenging position.
2. I wanted a position with more responsibility.
3. I wanted work that was career-oriented.
4. There was a general layoff in the plant.
5. The work was seasonal or part-time.
6. I became a full-time student.
7. I began a long-planned tour of the US.
8. I became self-employed.
9. I had an option for a better job.
10. I wanted to be more productive.
11. I wanted a job requiring my best skills.
12. I preferred a better work environment.
13. I made a long-planned move to this area (relocated).
14. I wanted a job in which I could learn.

Whenever possible, take an application home and fill it out at your leisure. Since this is not always feasible, be sure to carry with you all the data needed for a thorough and attractive application. Applications should be typed whenever possible. According to the Department of Labor and Statistics, over 80 percent of business executives who have received and viewed applications found most of them to be:

- Messy
- Incomplete
- Completed incorrectly
- All of the above

Some general tips the job seeker should take into consideration are the following:

1. *Carefully Follow Directions.* Did you write your application in cursive when it said to print? What about your name? Did you list your last name first as indicated? Work slowly so that you can do it right.

2. *Use a Black Ink Pen.* Never use pencil to fill out an application for employment; pencils do not look professional. The dull pencils that the personnel departments sometimes provide

for unprepared job seekers portray an unprepared job seeker's application. Using black ink pens portray a more professional appearance for the job seeker; you can even get black ink pens that can be erased just as easily as pencil. Bring two pens instead of one, just in case one stops working.

3. *Neatness is Mandatory.* Negative and messy applications for employment can get you screened out fast!

4. *Be Complete, Positive, and Honest.* Have all of your dates, phone numbers, and any other details that are often requested on applications prepared ahead of time. Again, do not leave blank spaces. If the question does not apply to you, write "N/A" (not applicable), or draw a line through it. In some instances, it may be important to state that you "will explain during the interview."

Parts of an Application

There are several basic parts of a job application (applications may vary, but they all have the same basic information).

They are as follows:
- Your identification
- Education and training
- Military experience
- Position desired
- Previous work experience
- References
- Miscellaneous information

The following pages show sample copies of incorrect and correct applications for employment. You may write out your own as well for a practice exercise in the blank form.

Correct Application for Employment

Name (last name first) **Smith Albert**
Date **April 1, 2011**
Soc. Sec. No. **846-44-1456**
Address **1526 North Otter Street**
Telephone **734-996-0721**
What kind of work are you applying for? **Assistant Manager**
What special qualifications do you have? **Extensive electrical and radio experience**
What office machines can you operate? **Business Machine**
Are you 18 years or older? Yes **X** No
Are you either a US citizen or an alien authorized to work in the United States? Yes **X** No

SPECIAL PURPOSE QUESTIONS

DO NOT ANSWER ANY OF THE QUESTIONS IN THIS FRAMED AREA UNLESS THE EMPLOYER HAS **CHECKED A BOX PRECEDING A** QUESTION, THEREBY INDICATING THAT THE INFORMATION IS REQUIRED FOR A BONA FIDE OCCUPATIONAL QUALIFICATION, OR DICTATED BY NATIONAL SECURITY LAWS, OR IS NEEDED FOR OTHER LEGALLY PERMISSIBLE REASONS.

☐ Height____Feet____Inches ☐ Weight____Lbs. ☒ Are you a US citizen? Yes____No____

☒ Have you been convicted of a felony or misdemeanor within the last 5 years?* Yes____No____Describe____

☐ I understand and agree that I may be required to take one or more: ☐ physical examination, ☐ lie detector test(s), as a condition of hiring or continued employment. I agree to consent to take such test(s) at such time as designated by the Company and to release the Company, its directors, officers, agents or employees from any claim arising in connection with the use of such test(s).

Yes____No____

☐ I have been advised that lie detector tests, as a condition of hiring or continued employment, are prohibited by law. Yes____No____

*You will not be denied employment solely because of a conviction record, unless the offense is related to the job for which you have applied.

MILITARY SERVICE RECORD

Branch of Service **United States Air Force** Discharge Date **1-2-94** Rank **E-2**
Present membership in National Guard or Reserves **X** Date obligation ends **4-15-94**

EDUCATION

SCHOOL	*NO. OF YEARS ATTENDED	NAME OF SCHOOL	CITY	COURSE	*DID YOU GRADUATE?
ELEMENTARY	6	Holy Trinity	Scon, PA	General	Ba
HIGH	3	Warren Central H.S.	Scon, PA	General	B
COLLEGE	3	University of Indpls.	Scon, PA	College Prep	Ba
OTHER					

* The Age Discrimination in Employment Act of 1967 prohibits discrimination on the basis of age with respect to individuals who are at least 40 years of age.

EXPERIENCE

NAME AND ADDRESS OF COMPANY	DATE FROM	DATE TO	LIST YOUR DUTIES	STARTING SALARY	FINAL SALARY	REASON FOR LEAVING
Ross Co.	8/97	10/98	Electrician	16,000.00	19,000.00	limited schedule
Scon Public Schools	7/96	3/97	Custodian Work	15,000.00	16,000.00	Desire a more demanding pos.
Wayne Construction	6/94	4/96	light construction work	14,000.00	15,000.00	Co. out of Business

BUSINESS REFERENCES

NAME	ADDRESS	OCCUPATION
Thomas Harrison	547 Detroit St. Scon, PA	Contractor
Marge Perkins	11645 Well St. Scon, PA	Electrician
Bob Parks	11712 Brod St. Scon, PA	Electrician

Incorrect Application for Employment

Name (last name first) _albert smith_   Date _april 1_

Address _1526 n. alder street_   Soc. Sec. No. _371-14-6E121_

Telephone _____

What kind of work are you applying for? _anything_

What special qualifications do you have? _Business_

What office machines can you operate? _none_

Are you 18 years or older? Yes _X_ No ____

Are you either a US citizen or an alien authorized to work in the United States? Yes _X_ No _____

SPECIAL PURPOSE QUESTIONS

DO NOT ANSWER **ANY** OF THE QUESTIONS IN THIS FRAMED AREA UNLESS THE EMPLOYER HAS **CHECKED A BOX PRECEDING A** QUESTION, THEREBY INDICATING THAT THE INFORMATION IS REQUIRED FOR A BONA FIDE OCCUPATIONAL QUALIFICATION, OR DICTATED BY NATIONAL SECURITY LAWS, OR IS NEEDED FOR OTHER LEGALLY PERMISSIBLE REASONS.

☐ Height ___ Feet ___ Inches ☐ Weight ___ Lbs. ☒ Are you a US citizen? Yes ___ No ___

☒ Have you been convicted of a felony or misdemeanor within the last 5 years?* Yes ___ No ___ Describe ___

☐ I understand and agree that I may be required to take one or more: ☐ physical examination; ☐ lie detector test(s), as a condition of hiring or continued employment. I agree to consent to take such test(s) at such time as designated by the Company and to release the Company, its directors, officers, agents or employees from any claim arising in connection with the use of such test(s).

Yes ___ No ___

☐ I have been advised that lie detector tests, as a condition of hiring or continued employment, are prohibited by law. Yes ___ No ___

*You will not be denied employment solely because of a conviction record, unless the offense is related to the job for which you have applied.

MILITARY SERVICE RECORD

Branch of Service _N/A_   Discharge Date _____   Rank _____

Present membership in National Guard or Reserves _____   Date obligation ends _____

EDUCATION

SCHOOL	*NO. OF YEARS ATTENDED	NAME OF SCHOOL	CITY	COURSE	*DID YOU GRADUATE?
ELEMENTARY	6	Holy Trinty	Scon, PA	Debreral	B
HIGH	3	Central H.S.	Scon, PA	General	B
COLLEGE	3	WCHS	Scon, PA	Col. Prep	C
OTHER					

* The Age Discrimination in Employment Act of 1967 prohibits discrimination on the basis of age with respect to individuals who are at least 40 years of age.

EXPERIENCE

NAME AND ADDRESS OF COMPANY	DATE FROM	DATE TO	LIST YOUR DUTIES	STARTING SALARY	FINAL SALARY	REASON FOR LEAVING
SPS	1996	1997	Cleaned up	8.00	9.00	Fired
Wayne conts	1983	1984	Jack hammer	7.00	8.00	Co. went broke
Central State Hosp.	1986	1986	hospitalized	6.00	7.00	got better

BUSINESS REFERENCES

NAME	ADDRESS	OCCUPATION
Thomas Harrison	?	Indust. worker
Marge Perkins	?	Electrical work
Bob Parks	?	Pub contractor

Sample Application for Employment

Date_____

Name (last name first)_____ Soc. Sec. No._____

Address_____ Telephone_____

What kind of work are you applying for?_____

What special qualifications do you have?_____

What office machines can you operate?_____

Are you 18 years or older?   Yes_____ No_____

Are you either a US citizen or an alien authorized to work in the United States?   Yes_____ No_____

SPECIAL PURPOSE QUESTIONS

DO NOT ANSWER **ANY** OF THE QUESTIONS IN THIS FRAMED AREA UNLESS THE EMPLOYER HAS **CHECKED A BOX PRECEDING** A QUESTION, THEREBY INDICATING THAT THE INFORMATION IS REQUIRED FOR A BONA FIDE OCCUPATIONAL QUALIFICATION, OR DICTATED BY NATIONAL SECURITY LAWS, OR IS NEEDED FOR OTHER LEGALLY PERMISSIBLE REASONS.

☐ Height_____Feet_____Inches   ☐ Weight_____Lbs.   ☒Are you a US citizen?   Yes_____ No_____

☒ Have you been convicted of a felony or misdemeanor within the last 5 years?*   Yes_____No_____Describe_____

☐ I understand and agree that I may be required to take one or more: ☐ physical examination; ☐ lie detector test(s), as a condition of hiring or continued employment. I agree to consent to take such test(s) at such time as designated by the Company and to release the Company, its directors, officers, agents or employees from any claim arising in connection with the use of such test(s).

Yes_____No_____

☐ I have been advised that lie detector tests, as a condition of hiring or continued employment, are prohibited by law.   Yes_____No_____

*You will not be denied employment solely because of a conviction record, unless the offense is related to the job for which you have applied.

MILITARY SERVICE RECORD

Branch of Service_____Discharge Date_____Rank_____

Present membership in National Guard or Reserves_____Date obligation ends_____

EDUCATION

SCHOOL	*NO OF YEARS ATTENDED	NAME OF SCHOOL	CITY	COURSE	*DID YOU GRADUATE?
ELEMENTARY					
HIGH					
COLLEGE					
OTHER					

* The Age Discrimination in Employment Act of 1967 prohibits discrimination on the basis of age with respect to individuals who are at least 40 years of age.

EXPERIENCE

NAME AND ADDRESS OF COMPANY	DATE		LIST YOUR DUTIES	STARTING SALARY	FINAL SALARY	REASON FOR LEAVING
	FROM	TO				

BUSINESS REFERENCES

NAME	ADDRESS	OCCUPATION

Chapter 11

The Interview Process

The definition of an interview is when you have a face-to-face discussion with a prospective employer about a position within a company. An interview can also be with an employer who does not currently have any job openings. There are many potential employers who are willing to interview you but do not have current job openings. However, you may be able to use these employers as a reference. Even though they may not hire people with your skills and background, they may know someone else who does. Hence, an interview with this kind of employer is appropriate.

When you are interviewing, you will find that most interviews last approximately 60 minutes, depending upon the level of responsibility involved, but it is the most important 60 minutes in your job search, so you should prepare accordingly. You will most likely have more than one interview, but each one is just as challenging as the one before, and you never know ahead of time which one will get you the job offer you have been eagerly expecting.

Most employers would agree that how well you do in an interview is crucial in determining whether or not you will be considered for a job. But remember, a successful interview does not always result in an offer for the job that you want! The interviewing process does not necessarily match you up with your ideal criteria, goals, or objectives. Furthermore, you may wish to be selective in accepting invitations for an interview. When you are looking for "that certain job," you may not want to spend your time and energy in "just any interview."

On the other hand, if you are an inexperienced job seeker, you may wish to participate in an interview just for practice, even though it involves a job in which you are not particularly interested. The more interviewing experiences you have, the more comfortable you will become with the interview process.

The ambitious job seeker who conducts a conventional job search is likely to experience frequent rejection, which, of course, could possibly cause anxiety. Eventually, the right opportunity will present itself, and when such an employer offers, that's a "Yes!" But along the way to that "yes" job offer, the feelings of rejection does not have to be one-sided. In other words, since the interview is a two-way communication, employers are not the only ones who can say "no."

Research the Organization First!

Listed below are things you might want to find out before you go to a job interview:

- **About the Organization**
  - Size—how many employees?
  - What percentage of employees are African-American?
  - What are their major products or services?
  - Who are their competitors? What is their competitive environment?
  - What are major changes in policies or status?
  - What kind of reputation and values do they portray?
  - What are the company's major weaknesses or opportunities?
  - Have there ever been any racial bias lawsuits (class-action)?
  - Are there any African-Americans in your managerial or partnership positions?

- **About the Interviewer**
  - What is his/her level and area of responsibility?
  - Does he or she have any special work-related projects, interests, or accomplishments?
  - What sort of boss is he or she?
  - What nationality is he or she?
  - What is his/her management style?

- **About the Position**
  - Have there ever been any African-Americans in the position you are seeking or in a similar position?
  - What openings or similar jobs now exist?
  - What has happened to others in similar positions?
  - What is the salary range and benefits?
  - What will my duties and responsibilities be?
  - What did the last person do wrong (for you to avoid it) or right (for you to emphasize it)?

Three Types Of Interviews

- Traditional Interview
- Information Interview
- Job Search Interview

Traditional Interview

The traditional interview will create a sense of fear and anxiety for most job seekers. Some of the fear and anxiety attacks result from something called "manipulation and counter-manipulation." Good interviewers will encourage you to be yourself and let your guard down. They know that if they tell you what they are looking for first, it will guide your responses, so they will try to keep you in the dark until they find out whether you are close to what they want. Even though some interviewers may not have formal training in interviewing, the very situation demands that they behave that way.

When there is a formal job opening, usually many people are interested, so the role of the interviewer is to weed out the "undesirables." Listed below are the most common methods used in traditional interviews:

One-On-One Interview   This interview is the most common type. During this interview, you may meet with a person whose role is to screen out applicants, select the best candidates, and arrange follow-up interviews with the person who has the authority to hire. Alternatively, you may meet directly with the person who has authority to hire.

Group Interview   In a group interview, you may be asked to interview with two or more people involved in the selection process. In some cases, the interviewer may choose to have a number of applicants interviewed at the same time.

Non-Directive Interview

In this interview session, interviewers may ask you an open-ended question that would encourage you to tell them whatever you want. For example, instead of asking you how well you did in school, they may ask, "What did you like best about school?" If you are not prepared for such questions, you may stumble into the wrong answer. A variety of responses to open-ended questions will be provided later, as well as techniques for handling almost any question.

Stress Interviews

Stress interviews are those in which the interviewer's intention is to try to get you upset. Interviewers using this technique hope to see how you are likely to react in pressure situations. For example, they might try to get you angry by not accepting something you say as true or by making subtle racial connotations. If that approach doesn't get you, perhaps some criticism will. Another approach is to quickly fire a question at you, but not give you time to completely answer, or to interrupt you mid-sentence. This is not nice, but you have been warned. If you run into this interview, be yourself and have a few laughs. The odds are the interview could turn out fine if you don't get upset and lose your composure. If you do get a job offer following such an interview, you might ask yourself if you want to work for such a company.

Structured Interviews	Structured interviews are becoming more and more common. This interviewing process is more prevalent in large organizations. The interviewer may have a list of things to ask and a form to fill out. Your experience and skills may be compared to specific job tasks or criteria. The interviewer will take notes. Even if the interview is highly structured, you will usually have the opportunity to present what you feel is essential about yourself.
Disorganized Interviews	Let's face it, you will come across some interviewers who simply will not know how to interview you. They may talk about themselves too much or neglect to ask you any meaningful questions. Some people are competent managers but poor interviewers.

Informational Interview

Basically, the informational interview is the potential employee's gathering and organization of data. Rather than being initiated by the potential employer, it is an assessment technique used by job seekers to help them identify their job objectives. To effectively use this technique, you must first have done your homework. You must know your skills and select the ones you really want to use in your next job. You must also decide on a variety of other factors you want in your "ideal" job: size and type of organization, salary level, interests, what sort of co-workers, and other preferences.

The next step is to gather data on where your "ideal" job might exist and what it might be called. People who use this interview technique correctly often receive a warm welcome when they ask someone to help them out.

If you are truly honest and sincere about this interview technique, and you do your homework before using this method (seeking information and not a job), then the technique is both effective and fun. You get a chance to meet lots of people and learn all sorts of things about whatever it is you want to know. Each person will refer you to someone else who knows more, and you will gradually narrow down the field to positions very close to your ideal one. This wonderful technique, unfortunately, has been misused and abused. Those individuals who really wanted to get a specific job have used the technique as a trick to get in to see someone ("I'm not looking for a job, but I am conducting a survey..."). Most employers know dishonesty when they see it, and many employers are very uncertain about even the sincere people asking to see them for any reason.

Richard Bolles laments this and indicates that some trainers and others who should know better have encouraged this dishonesty. He does point out, however, that the technique is still useful, particularly outside of larger cities and with smaller organizations.

Job Search Interview

The job search interview is as follows:

- You know what sort of job you want.
- You know why someone should hire you to do it.
- You can communicate clearly and comfortably to someone else.

The interviewer knows something about the sort of job you are looking for, or at the very least, knows other people whom may know.

The Interview Process

Step I: Before You Formally Meet the Interviewer: He/she has already created an impression of you. If it's bad, nothing good can come of it.

Step II: Opening Introduction: The interview process is not a game, but how you begin it will determine whether you win or lose.

Step III: The Interview: This is the most important part of the whole process. It is here that you will have an opportunity to present your skills in response to the questions. But the impression you make here is highly determined by how well you communicate your skills and abilities.

Step IV: The Closing of an Interview: There is more to ending an interview than saying a simple goodbye.

Step V: The Follow-Up: You must send a thank-you note. People who follow up and follow through get jobs over those who do not. It's that simple!

Step VI: The Negotiation: This could happen during your first interview, or any subsequent interviews, but knowing what to do, and how, can make it all worthwhile.

Step VII: The Final Decision: Sometimes saying "no" to a job offer may be the best thing you could do for yourself, even though you have worked hard at the job offer. Sometimes saying no will provide you with a decision-making process that will help you evaluate important life decisions.

Most Frequently Asked Interview Questions

Practicing answers to frequently asked interview questions will not only prepare you to answer these questions effectively, but also prepare you to answer other interview questions.

Because each person is different, each response is different during an interview. There is no one correct way to answer an interview question. To help you develop your own responses, though, let's analyze some frequently-asked interview questions and reveal their underlying meanings. Strategies for answering the questions will be provided, and sample responses will be given. You can then write down your own brief responses as well.

1. Why should I hire you?

    In answering this question, you must always focus on the advantage of hiring you. This involves providing the potential employer with proof that you can help them make more money. Explain how you could improve their company's services. Reducing costs, increasing sales, and solving customer service problems are skills that the employer wants. You must remember that the bottom line is the needs of the employer.

2. What are your future plans?

    The employer would like to explore how long you might stay with the company. This question is an attempt to find out whether or not you can be depended upon, and how much time to spend training you. The employer, in other words, is attempting to find out the following information:

    ■ Will you be happy with the salary? (If not, you might leave).

    ■ Will you leave for a new job or to raise a family?

    ■ Do you have a history of leaving jobs after a short period of time?

    ■ If you have just moved to the area, are you a temporary resident or transient?

    ■ Are you overqualified?

- Do you have the energy and commitment to advance in this job?

- Could you become dissatisfied with this job?

- Have you been released from a prior position because you were too outspoken?

3. What are your strengths and weaknesses?

This question has hidden meaning. Your answer should always emphasize your transfer and maintenance skills. The decision to hire you will be based on these skills. You can specify job-related skills later on during the interview. Always remember, though, your answer should be brief.

Below is a response from a person who has little prior work experience:

"One of my major strengths is my ability to work hard toward a goal. Once I decide to do something, it will probably get done. For example, I graduated from high school four years ago. Many of my friends started working and others went on to school. At the time I didn't know what I wanted to do, so going on to school did not make sense. The jobs I could get at the time didn't excite me either, so I looked into joining the Service. I took the test and discovered a few things about myself that surprised me. For one thing, I was much better at understanding complex problems than my grades in high school would suggest. I signed up for a three-year hitch that included intensive training in electronics. I worked hard and graduated in the top 20 percent of my class!

I was then assigned to monitor, diagnose, and repair an advanced electronics system that was worth about two million dollars. I was promoted several times to the position of E4, which is the rank of sergeant, and received an honorable discharge after my tour of duty.

> I now know what I want to do and am prepared to spend extra time learning whatever is needed to do well"

A weakness can be used to your advantage by turning it into a strength:

> "I have been accused by my coworkers of being too involved in my work. I usually come in a little early to organize my day and stay late to get a project done on time. I need to learn to be more patient. I often do things myself just because I know I can do them faster and better than someone else. This has not let me be as good as I want to be at delegating things for others to do, but I am working on it. I'm now spending more time showing others how to do the things I want done, and that has helped. They often do better than I expect if I am clear enough with what I want done and how".

4. Tell me (a little bit) about yourself

    Interviewers may ask this question in a direct way. A casual, friendly conversation would sometimes provide them with the information they need. In most cases, the interviewer is seeking information that would indicate whether you are stable or unpredictable. For example:

    > "After high school, I worked in a variety of business settings and learned a great deal about how various businesses run. For example, I was given complete responsibility for the daily operations of a wholesale distribution company that grossed over $2 million a year. That was only three years after I graduated from high school. There, I learned to supervise other people and solve problems under pressure. I also got more interested in the financial end of running a business and decided, after three years and three promotions, to go after a position where I could have more involvement in key strategies and long-term management decisions".

5. Why did you leave your last job?

   Sometimes employers will ask this questions just to find out if you had any problems at your last job. If you did, you may have the same problems at a new job (they would think). The following are some suggestions on how to answer this question:

   ■ Never say anything negative about your previous employer or even about yourself. If you had problems on your last job, explain them in a way that is not negative (refer to "Positive Reasons for Leaving a Job").

   ■ Never use the word "fired" or "terminated" to explain why you left your previous job. Perhaps you were returning to school or were laid off. Use positive words or phrases to describe what happened.

   ■ If you were in fact fired and/or not on good terms with previous employers, this should be explained during your interview. Examine first why you were fired. Did you learn something from the situation? Were you to blame as well?

   ■ Avoid criticizing your previous employer. If you have learned something from the situation with your previous employer, explain this honestly. Many people get fired from their jobs at some time in their lives. The odds are great that your interviewer may understand your situation better than you expect. Sometimes people are fired because of personal reasons that interfere with their work. Did you have car problems? A divorce? Or something even more personally devastating in your life? Have you resolved the problem? If so, inform the interviewer of this. Tell the interviewer that the previous problem has been resolved and will not affect your work.

6. How much experience do you have?

   This question requires a direct response. It relates to your credentials. Your response will be very important if you have created a good impression so far. You have to overcome any weakness that you may have. Your background will be compared to those of other job seekers. If it appears that others may have more education or more years of experience than you, acknowledge that and present your strengths. For example:

> "As you know, I have just completed an intensive program in the area of computer programming. In addition, I have over three years of work experience in a variety of business settings. That work experience includes managing a small business during the absence of the owner. There, I learned to handle money and a variety of basic bookkeeping tasks. I also inventoried and organized products worth over $300,000. These experiences have helped me understand the consequences of computer programming in a business setting. While I am new to the career of programming, I am familiar with the language used by your equipment. My educational experience was very thorough, and I have over three hundred hours of interactive computer time as part of my coursework. Because I am new, I plan to work harder and will spend personal time as needed to meet any necessary deadlines required on the job".

7. What are your pay expectations?

The real purpose of this question is to help the employer either eliminate you from consideration or save money at your expense. Your objective, though, is to create a positive impression during this initial interview. Here are some things you could say:

- What is the salary range that you normally would pay for this position or other positions that are similar to this one?

- I am very much interested in the position, and my salary would be open for negotiation.

- What do you have in mind for the salary range?

8. Why did you choose this field?

   Employers want to know if you are just looking for a job. They are much more interested in people who are interested in a career. They assume that this kind of person will work harder and be more productive. People who have a good reason for seeking the position will be seen as more organized, more committed, and more likely to stay on the job longer.

   An example statement would be:

   > "I realize I need to establish myself in this field, but I am very willing to get started. I've thought about what I want to do, and I am very sure my skills are the right ones to do well in this career. For example, I am good at dealing with people. In one position, I provided services to over 1,000 different people a week. During the 18 months I was there, I served well over 72,000 customers and not once did I get a formal complaint. In fact, I was often complimented on the attention I gave them. I learned that there I enjoy public contact and I am delighted at the idea of this position for that reason. I want to learn more about the business and grow with it. As my contributions and value to the organization increase, I hope to be considered for more responsible positions".

9. Why did you choose this company?

   Demonstrate that you are a good match for the company. Explain your:

   ■ Motivation for selecting this career goal

   ■ Special skills that are a perfect match for the position

   ■ Training and credentials that are necessary for the position

10. What are your likes and dislikes?

    In most cases, when interviewers ask this question, they seek information that may indicate if you are unstable or undependable. Sometimes the interviewer will get this information through a casual, friendly conversation.

    If asked this question, describe your likes and dislikes in a positive statement, such as: "I like things to run in a smooth and organized manner. I dislike my working area when it is kept in a disorganized and unclean condition."

Answering Problem Questions

(How to Handle Illegal Questions)

On occasion, potential employers ask illegal questions without realizing they are doing so. Some interviewers, in fact, are not aware of laws regarding the questioning of a prospective employee. In general, your interviewer should not ask questions or make comments about your sex, marital status, race, color, religion, housing, physical data (age, weight, height, etc.), or handicaps.

You have three options when confronted with illegal interview questions:

1. You could answer the questions and simply ignore the fact that they are illegal.

2. You could ask, "Could you tell me why you are asking that question?" Then upon hearing the interviewer's response, decide whether or not to answer.

3. Contact the nearest civil rights office. Be aware, however, that even though you may have a legitimate claim, it may be difficult to prove that you have been a victim of discrimination.

Whatever you choose to do, pause to consider whether or not you would want to work for an employer who asks illegal questions. After you have been hired, however, there are some statistical data that the employer may need, such as your marital status and the names and ages of your children, for federal and state tax and insurance purposes.

Questions to Ask the Interviewer

Just as we expect the interviewer to ask a variety of questions during the employment interview, the prospective employer expects you to ask questions. Remember, you are also trying to decide whether or not you will accept a job if it is offered. The employer realizes this. He or she will be glad to know that you are interested and trying to make a good decision.

Here are some questions you may want to ask if the employer has not already offered the answer.

- What do you look for in an employee?
- What are the job duties?
- What are the fringe benefits?
- What are the hours?
- What are the opportunities for advancement?
- What are the opportunities for on-the-job training and further education?
- What is the salary range for this position?
- Is there any traveling involved?
- Are there parking facilities?
- Is employment contingent upon annual funding by an outside source?
- How often are employees evaluated and by what method?
- Who will be my supervisor? (Or ask to be shown your position on the company's organizational chart.)

Negotiate Your Salary

Never discuss salary until the position has been offered. Discussing salary too early could be a big stumbling block to getting the job. You want the employer to believe that you are genuinely interested in the job and its responsibilities, but do not accept a job without knowing the salary. Know what you would like your salary to be before you go into an interview and work toward that goal.

Before discussing salary requirements with your potential employer, remember first to:

1. Research the salary range for the position you are considering, or similar positions. You can do this through trade journals (which compile salary surveys for various industries), trade associations, asking others in the field, and checking the classified ads (which oftentimes will list salaries along with job requirements).

2. Make an inquiry into what the person who had the job before was paid.

3. Decide if this job is a good stepping stone into your career or whether or not salary is an important issue to you at this stage in your career.

4. Some jobs have very flexible salaries, and some do not. Try to determine which category your position falls into. Jobs that require more advanced skills usually have more pay flexibility, and jobs that require fewer skills will probably have less pay flexibility.

5. Consider the state of the local economy during your salary negotiation. If the economy is weak, your negotiating power will be weak. If the economy is strong, your negotiating power will also be strong.

6. Determine the demand for your skills if you have highly specialized skills, you may have an edge in negotiation. If your skills are more generalized and shared by other applicants, you may not.

7. During salary negotiation:

- Always let the employer suggest the first salary, and keep in mind that the initial offer is most likely below what the company is actually willing to pay.

- If you must indicate your salary requirements, give a salary range you would consider. Try to watch the employer's body language and overall response to judge whether your range is in the ballpark. Remember, too, that employers are good actors when it comes to negotiating salaries.

- Always be firm when stating your salary requirements. Never let the employer think you're wishy-washy about salary. For example, say, "I want 'x,'" instead of, "Well, this may be too much, but I'd like to make 'x' amount. Is that a problem?"

- Never accept a salary that the employer first offers. Respond with, "I was hoping for something closer to 'x.'" Make sure that your "x" amount is higher than what you think you can get. This will leave room for compromise.

- Your options for discussing salary could be in weekly, monthly, or annual terms, so long as you understand how the numbers add up or break down.

- Sometimes the employer may ask you how much you made at your previous job. Try to avoid the question, especially if you are seeking a large hike in pay. If you have to answer, answer honestly, explaining that your responsibilities in this new position sound like they would be much more challenging and worthy of a higher salary.

- Ask how often salary reviews are given.

- Find out how much the raises generally increase when they're given. Remember some employers may exaggerate this claim.

- Never accept less now if the employer suggests to you that you can renegotiate your salary in three to six months when you've proved yourself. You'll have no leverage by that time.

- Think about whether you can, in fact, afford to live on the salary being offered. Be sure to account for state and federal taxes, which comes out of your pay. Remember that the cost of living varies from state to state. For example, a terrific salary for Kansas City might be impossible to live on in New York City.

- Take into consideration benefits such as health insurance, stock options, and vacation time.

- Find out if your health insurance is deducted from your salary, and if so, what amount.

- When negotiating salary, always focus on the qualities that you will be bringing to the job rather than the salary. The key is to make the employer feel that you are worth the salary that you want.

- Always get everything in writing. For example, "We will be reviewing your salary in six months," etc.

- Never consider overtime or bonuses, such as Christmas bonuses, as part of your salary package. Bonuses are always considered to be at the discretion of the employer when the company is doing exceptionally well. You don't want to wait for Christmas to get your money.

- Always get realistic expectations if a commission is part of your salary. The employer will most likely highlight earnings of people who make the most in commissions while downplaying those people who earn average or below-average commissions.

- If the employer becomes extremely aggressive in discussing of salary, ask whether you can think about the salary and get back to him or her later. This will provide an opportunity for tensions to subside and for you to assess your options.

Evaluating Healthcare Plans

When you consider a position, make sure you are informed as to whether or not your compensation package includes a healthcare plan. Keep in mind that employer-provided healthcare programs can provide varied coverage at differing costs. Find out what type of plan, if any, your new employer offers. Determine if you have to pay certain deductibles. Ask if you will be contributing to the plan in the form of a monthly premium, since some employers pay only a portion of their employee's premiums. Find out if the plan includes life insurance. If you're single with no dependents, this factor will probably be less important to you than if you have a spouse and children. Some of the most common plans being offered by today's employers are:

- Indemnity Insurance
- Preferred Provider Organization
- Exclusive Provider Organization
- Health Maintenance Organization (HMO)
- Open-Ended Health Maintenance Organization

Indemnity Insurance

For years, this program has been the mainstay of the benefit programs for American business. Recently, though, other options have surfaced and have gained in popularity. Under the indemnity insurance, you can choose your own doctors and hospitals. You pay an annual deductible (ranging from $100 to $300), after which the insurance pays for 80 percent of the medical bills, and you pay the remaining 20 percent. These plans do not cover preventative care, such as physical exams or immunizations.

Preferred Provider Organization

This plan is part of the indemnity plan, and covers most healthcare costs if the employee goes to a selected doctor or a hospital that has agreed to provide services at a discount. This plan features little or no deductible and often pays as much as 90-100 percent of the cost. You may only go to selected healthcare providers or you will pay increased fees and deductibles. You may also be required to obtain pre-approval for a hospital admission.

Exclusive Provider Organization

This is similar to a preferred provider organization but has additional restrictions. You choose from a list of primary care physicians who determine whether or not you need to see a specialist and who monitors all treatment you will receive. This plan is based on the primary care physician overseeing and protecting the insured from receiving any unnecessary treatment.

Health Maintenance Organization

These are referred to as HMO's. They have gained popularity in recent years because they emphasize preventative care. Other insurance plans pay for medical bills only after they have been incurred by the patient; on the other hand, HMO's operate on a prepaid agreement to provide health care. You are assigned to a doctor who provides primary care, and who will also decide when you need to see a specialist. You pay a small co-payment of $5 to $30 for each doctor visit.

Sometimes, HMO's will actually employ the doctor and own the hospital where patients receive treatment. In other cases, HMO's contract with doctors and clinics to provide health care to HMO members. These IPA's (Independent Practice Associations, as they are commonly called) are paid a set monthly free per patient, whether or not the patient requires health services.

Open-Ended Health Maintenance Organization

This is a plan which combines components from HMO and insurance plans. You sign up with an HMO and seek alternative health care for a co-payment of 20-30 percent, with a deductible of $100 to $500.

Closing an Interview

1. Thank the interviewer by name.

   "I would like to thank you, Mr./Mrs. , for the interview time."

2. State that you are interested in the job.

   "I want to let you know that I am very interested in this position."

3. Show interest in the company.

   "...and working for this company."

4. State that you are able do the job.

   "I know I have the skills to do a good job for you."

5. Indicate that you will be busy.

   "...but I'm going to be busy and have other appointments to set up."

6. Request the chance to contact them.

   "What I'd like to do is schedule a time to call you back."

7. Indicate a reason for the call-back.

   "...to ask you any other questions I might have and answer any others you might have."

8. Get call-back date and time.

   "When is the best time for me to do this? The beginning or the end of the week? The morning or the afternoon?"

9. Thank the interviewer and assure him/her of the call-back.

   "I want to thank you again, and I will be calling with questions."

10. Send a thank-you note.

    As soon as possible, send a simple thank-you note specifying your interest in the job and your ability to do good work.

Chapter 12

How to Evaluate Job Offers

Choosing the best job offer for yourself is just as important as the interview and the job-hunt. You may have several job offers, so it is wise to pick the one that best fits your needs.

The chart on the following page outlines some job variables that you may want to consider when you make your job choice.

Organizing Your Job Offer Evaluations

	Company One	Company Two	Company Three
1. Company name			
2. Company benefits offered			
3. Challenging?			
4. Creativity			
5. Good Schedule			
6. Status			
7. Title			
8. Satisfactory responsibility			
9. Salary			
10. Acceptable location			
11. Good work environment			
12. Training			
13. Educational opportunities			
14. Acceptable supervision			
15. Promotional opportunities			
16. Flexibility			
Total Ranking			

Fill in the blanks with numbers or "yes"/"no," then rank each job variable by importance to you. Circle your top five variables, taking into consideration any other variables that are not listed here. Once you have finalized your five most important job variables, carefully consider what is important to you. The company scoring highest in your top variables is probably your best job option.

Chapter 13

Your First Week at Your New Job

Your first week on the job may involve a series of ups and downs, successes and failures. Listed below are several positive strategies that will help you create a solid beginning.

- Learn your new job
- Be on time
- Respect your co-workers and superiors and earn their respect
- Make a good impression
- Use proper phone manners
- Greet people properly
- Avoid profanity and slang language
- Always dress for success
- Be organized
- Keep your work space professional looking

Remember, you won't be new forever. Again, always portray a positive attitude on your new job. When you display this positive attitude with enthusiasm for the job and a desire to learn more, you will be a more likely candidate for job advancement.

Chapter 14

Keeping Your Job!

Your first 90 days on the job are very critical and the most difficult. Your boss will be paying close attention to you during this time. Many companies practice the 90-day probation period for new employees.

This period seems to be the most difficult for new employees. As a new employee, you are changing your life, learning a new job, and working with new people. You must apply yourself from day one. Learn everything as accurately as you can, and complete every task. Help other employees when it is necessary, and if you are recommended for a training program, pay attention, participate, and ask questions.

A survey of over 500 employers located across the United States was conducted to identify what employers in business, industry, and government value in prospective employees. The employers were asked, "How important are the following factors when evaluating the performance of new employees in your organization?

Out of 70 factors, the following items were ranked the most important.

1. Ability to get things done
2. Common sense
3. Honesty/Integrity
4. Dependability
5. Initiative
6. Well-developed work habits
7. Reliability
8. Interpersonal skills
9. Enthusiasm
10. Motivation to achieve
11. Adaptability
12. Intelligence
13. Decision-making skills
14. Energy level
15. Problem-solving abilities
16. Attitude toward workplace
17. Mental alertness
18. Emotional control

After your first 90 days, your employer may give you a formal review, and your supervisor will tell you whether or not you have done well or poorly, and whether you should improve. So, prepare yourself to accept criticism, and work to improve.

Listed on the following page are 20 reasons that are within a worker's control to avoid being fired and 20 reasons that are outside a worker's control to avoid being fired. In addition to these, each company has its own rules and regulations. Once you are hired, you should find out what your company's rules and regulations are and make sure not to break them. Your job is at stake; don't lose it!

Do's and Don'ts for the New Employee

Reasons Within a New Employee's Control

1. Absence or being late for work without just cause. Chronic recurrence of this means an added burden on fellow workers. It shows a lack of concern about the job and its duties.

2. Being accident-prone. This is a danger to self and others. It results in excessive absenteeism and increases insurance costs.

3. Ambition (too little, or too much). Too little ambition means the worker is inefficient, lacks drive, and is disoriented. Too much ambition causes dissension and jealousy among co-workers as the relentless drive to reach the top of the ladder is pursued. There is a tendency to overact, create ill will, and become domineering.

4. Attention to outside interests. Using company time and facilities to further personal off-the-job interests. The quality of work goes down, and the employee becomes limited in his value to the employer. This is actually a form of cheating.

5. Taking excessive coffee/lunch breaks.

6. Maintaining a messy work area.

7. Smoking in the "No Smoking" areas.

8. Disloyalty. This could include slander against supervisors or company executives, divulging trade secrets or processes, or talking too much about the happenings of the job or its functions.

9. Horseplay. This could include fooling around on the job, not tending to assigned duties, distracting others or engaging in practical jokes that cause accidents or injury, resulting in losses of time.

10. Going to sleep while you're at work.

11. Insubordination. This could include disrespect to supervisors, to the company, or to fellow workers. Domestic or emotional problems could cause this.

12. Irresponsibility. This could include failing to complete assigned tasks, being haphazard in conduct and attitude, and having sloppy work habits.

13. Lack of adaptability. This could include being unwilling to adapt to concepts, being stalemated in a routine which has become a habit, or adopting a "You Can't Teach an Old Dog New Tricks" attitude.

14. Stealing company supplies, tools, or equipment.

15. Lying. This could include false or exaggerated statements on the employment application. Lying about mistakes on the job is a disservice to the company. When the supervisor investigates an error, it is not for the purpose of fixing blame on any person. He or she must know what went wrong, if anyone is at fault, if the procedures can be corrected, and if he or she must implement ways to prevent a recurrence. To lie or to blame someone else for your errors is a serious offense.

16. Laziness. This could include doing just barely enough to slip under the wire.

17. Misrepresentation. This could include trying to portray an image of oneself that is different from one's actual personality.

18. Objection to transfer or promotion. This could include refusal to relocate to another department or area or refusing a promotion because it may mean travel or relocation.

19. Leaving the facility during working hours without permission.

20. Getting convicted of a criminal offense other than a minor traffic violation.

Reasons Outside a New Employee's Control

1. Acts of God. These could include fire, flood, hurricane, tornado, earthquake, etc.

2. Bankruptcy. The company's liabilities exceed its assets.

3. Cancellation of orders. This often affects workers hired for proposed work loads that did not materialize.

4. Competition for orders. Other companies may possess better products, lower prices, more effective marketing techniques, greater acceptance, a higher degree of efficiency, or better cost reduction control.

5. Completion of work. When the job is done, workers are not needed. Construction is one example.

6. Decreased demand. Customers may no longer be buying the product or service (there are many reasons for this).

7. Economic depression. People can't afford the product or service.

8. Discrimination. This might involve issues of age, sex, religion, race, nationality, or disability status.

9. Economic changes. Certain industries may change adversely (aerospace industries, space programs, and electronics are examples), which will affect the entire national economy to some degree.

10. Legislation. A product may be outlawed or restricted by law, or price controls may be in effect.

11. Management incompetence. This may result in inefficiency, waste, excessive manpower, inadequate manpower, dishonesty, or poor management techniques.

12. Merger. This could result in having only key personnel remain.

13. Nepotism. This involves hiring of relatives and friends.

14. Obsolescence. This occurs when the product or service is no longer useful.

15. Declining profits. Insufficient profit may make it impossible to maintain operations (meat packers, and gasoline distributors are good examples).

16. Economic recession. Consumers may be spending more wisely, especially if the product or service is not a necessity of life.

17. Seniority rights. This can result in being bumped off the job by someone with greater seniority because of the rules of unions and management.

18. Stockholders. They have the power to dictate new policies.

19. Strikes. They may result from bargaining and communications breakdowns between management and unions.

20. Taxes. They may cut too far and deep into profits to make the operation feasible.

Attitudes

Your attitude plays an important role in your work environment. In a recent survey, employers were asked what they considered to be the most important qualification in a new employee. Job skills were not at the top of the list; instead, employers ranked appearance, attitude, dependability, reliability, honesty, and a willingness to learn as the most important!

Employers also maintain that poor attitudes are one of the main reasons why people don't get hired. Below are three exercises in dealing with attitudes. Write down for each employment scenario what you would do if these incidents were to happen to you. There is no one correct answer. Discuss your ideas with your friends, classmates, or family. Do you know of any one that has encountered such problems?

1. Takwana David, a new employee, has been working on an assembly line for one week. She enjoys her work and wants to show her supervisor that she will be a reliable employee. Therefore, Mary has been working at a consistently high rate. Her co-workers do not put as much effort into their work. They are beginning to harass Mary because she assembles more parts than they, and they feel threatened. Mary feels she should do her best and give her employer a full day's work for a full day's pay, yet she wants to have a good relationship with her co-workers. What should she do?

2. Frank Jenkins is an assistant warehouse manager for a rather large automotive supply house. Because he knows all of his jobs so well, he sometimes finds himself doing most of them. He works hard and frequently works overtime. The warehouse manager recently started giving David jobs that could be done by one of the newer men. These extra jobs leave David with too little time to do his regular job. In short, David feels that he gets the jobs simply because the manager does not want to train one of the new men to do them. All of the work assignments are made by the warehouse manager. How can David solve this problem and get the job done effectively?

3. Joanna has been working in shipping and receiving for two years. She has been with the company for a total of nine years. She enjoys her work immensely and has been happy working there. About one year ago, Mrs. Benson was hired. Mrs. Benson is not Joanna's supervisor, but she is related to Mr. Harper, who is Joanna's boss. Mrs. Benson acts as though she is Joanna's boss, criticizing her often and complaining to Mr. Harper about her. Yesterday, Joanna left work early for a dentist appointment, after first making suitable arrangements with Mr. Harper. The next day, when Joanna came in, Mrs. Benson came up to her and said, "An extra crew is needed to work overtime on Saturday. I volunteered you to work. Be here at 8:00." For Joanna, this was the last straw. What should she do?

You now know what your employers expect from you on the job, and you know what will get you fired. But it's also easy to stay hired. Good luck!

Chapter 15

Distinct Qualities of Successful People

In studying the lives of successful people, one would discover certain character traits that are common to virtually all of them.

Perhaps you know of someone who possesses outstanding character traits.

1. Write a short paragraph describing the most successful person you know.

2. List four outstanding qualities that you believe helped this individual achieve success.

3. On a scale from 1 to 10, rate yourself on these same four qualities.

The four common quality character traits most listed are:

- Confidence
- Perseverance
- Hard work
- Courage

Are these the same traits you listed? Having confidence in yourself will provide you with the courage to implement a successful job search. To persevere, you may need to work even harder than you've ever worked on a job. However, your working hard should eventually spell success in your search for a new job.

Chapter 16

The Job Search Quiz

As a job seeker, you must be aware of changing conditions in the job market. The Job Search Quiz is designed to give you a better understanding of the job market.

1. List the five most important reasons why you believe people stay unemployed.

    a.

    b.

    c.

    d.

    e.

2. What are the three most important criteria that employers use to screen out (disqualify) a job seeker?

   a.

   b.

   c.

3. The average length of time a job seeker is unemployed is:

   _____

4. List five of your most important skills.
   (They do not necessarily have to be job-related. They should be things you think you can do particularly well.)

   a.

   b.

   c.

   d.

   e.

5. What are the two most common ways to locate jobs?

   a.

   b.

6. How many job search hours should you invest?

   _____

7. How often does the average person change jobs?

   _____

8. How often does the average person change careers in a lifetime?

    _____

9. Jobs are advertised _____% of the time.

10. The purpose of an application form is to

    _____.

11. Do large businesses hire most job seekers?

    Why?_____

12. What is the current unemployment rate in your region (an estimated percentage)?_____

Answers To The Job Search Quiz

1. a. Appearance
   b. Cannot describe their skills (80 percent of all people who are looking for a job cannot adequately describe their skills to the interviewer)
   c. Cannot answer problem questions
   d. Do not look/search hard enough
   e. Job-seekers do not know how to look for job openings

2. a. Appearance
   b. Dependability
   c. Skills

3. The average number of weeks a job-seeker is unemployed varies, according to the US Department of Labor, which keeps track of such figures annually.

4. This question will vary, according to the individual. People who can tell employers what their skills are and how they can help them do the job that they are interviewing for tend to get hired over others. Many people have trouble identifying their skills, but it is essential that you answer this question accurately and completely.

5. a. Contact employers directly

   b. Obtain job leads from friends and relatives and follow up on those leads

6. Twenty-five to forty hours of job-seeking per week is not unreasonable.

7. Minorities and younger workers, on the average, change jobs more often and are more frequently unemployed. On average, 20 percent of the working population experiences some unemployment. According to the US Department of Labor and Statistics, persons under the age of 35 change jobs every year and a half. Those persons aged 35 and over change jobs less frequently, averaging one job-change every three years.

8. The average person changes careers every six to eight years.

9. Twenty-five percent of all jobs are advertised.

10. To screened out applicants.

11. Small organizations tend to create new jobs for new workers.

12. The current unemployment rate varies according to region; contact your local state employment office for specific details. However, a significant percentage of unemployment in any region is based on:

    ■ First-time job-seekers
    ■ Those looking for seasonal and part-time employment
    ■ People that are re-entering the workforce
    ■ Others who do not have a pending economic need for employment

References

State Directors of Adult Education

If you have difficulty at your state office then contact the Federal headquarters at Clearinghouse on Adult Education and Literacy, Division of Adult Education and Literacy, U.S. Department of Education, 400 Maryland Ave., SW, Washington, DC 20202; 202-205-9996.

Alabama
State Administrator
GED Testing Program
Adult Basic Education Section
Division of Federal Administrative
Services
Department of Education
Gordon Parsons Building, Rm. 5343
50 North Ripley Street
Montgomery, AL 36130
334-242-8181
Fax: 334-242-2236

Alaska
State Supervisor, Adult Basic
Education
Department of Education
801 West 10th, Box F
Juneau, AK 99801
907-465-3396

Arizona
State Administrator
Adult Education Services
Department of Education
1535 West Jefferson
Phoenix, AR 85007
602-542-1849

Arkansas
Deputy Director
Adult Education Section
Department of Education
Luther S. Hardin Building, #506
Third Capitol Mall
Little Rock, AR 72201-1083
501-682-1970/1978
Fax: 501-682-1982

California
State Director
Adult Education
Department of Education
P.O. Box 944272
Sacramento, CA 942244-2720
916-322-6535
Fax: 916-327-4239

Colorado
State Director, ABE
Division of Adult Education
201 E. Colfax Avenue
Denver, CO 80203
303-866-6611
Fax: 303-830-0793

Connecticut

Director, Division of Vocational Technical and Adult Education
Department of Education
25 Industrial Park Rd.
Middletown, CT 06457
203-638-4035
Fax: 203-638-4156/4062

Delaware

State Supervisor
Adult and Community Education
Department of Public Instruction
P.O. Box 1402
J.G. Townsend Building
Dover, DE 19901
302-739-4681
Fax: 302-739-3744

District of Columbia

Assistant Superintendent
District of Columbia Public Schools
Browne Administrative Unit
26th and Benning Rd., NE
Washington, DC 20002
202-724-4178
Fax: 202-724-4750

Florida

Bureau of Adult and Community Education
FEC Building
Department of Education
325 W. Gains Street
Room 1244
Tallahassee, FL 32399-0400
904-487-4929
Fax: 904-487-6259

Georgia

Assistant Commissioner for Adult Literacy
Department of Technical and A.E.
1800 Centary Place
Atlanta, GA 30345-4304
404-679-1635
Fax: 404-679—1630

Hawaii

Administrator, Youth and Early Childhood Section
Department of Education
Hahaione Elementary School
595 Pepeekeo St., H-2
Honolulu, HI 96825
808-395-9451
Fax: 808-395-1826

Idaho

Director Adult Education
Department of Education
Len B. Jordon Office Building
650 W. State Street
Boise, ID 83720
208-334-2187
Fax: 208-334-2228

Illinois

Director of Adult Education
Adult, Vocational and Technical Education
State Board of Education
100 N. First St., E-439
Springfield, IL 62777
217-782-3370
Fax: 217-782-9224

Indiana

Director, Division of Adult Education
Department of Education
Room 229, State House
Indianapolis, IN 46204
317-232-0522
Fax: 317-232-9121

Iowa

Chief, Adult Education
Department of Education
Grimes State Office Building
Des Moines, IA 50319-0146
515-281-3671
Fax: 515-242-5988

Kansas

Director, Adult Education
Department of Education
120 East 10th Street
Topeka, KS 66612
913-296-3191
Fax: 913-296-7933

Kentucky

Office Head
Adult Education Services
Department of Adult and Technical
Education
Capital Plaza Tower, 3rd Floor
500 Mero Street
Frankfort, KY 40601
502-564-5114
Fax: 502-564-5316

Louisiana

Director, Bureau of Adult and Com-
munity Education
Department of Education
P.O. Box 94064
Baton Rouge, LA 70804-9064
504-342-3510
Fax: 504-342-7316

Maine

Adult and Community Education
Department of Education
State House Station 23
Augusta, ME 04333
207-289-5854
Fax: 207-287-5894

Maryland

Adult Education and Literacy Services
Branch
Division of Career Technology and
Adult Learning, 3rd Floor
Maryland State Department of
Education
200 West Baltimore Street
Baltimore, MD 21201
410-767-0162
Fax: 410-333-2379

Massachusetts

Adult and Community Service
Department of Education
350 Main Street, 4th Floor
Malden, MA 02148
617-388-3300 ext. 353
Fax: 617-388-3394

Michigan

Adult Extended Learning Services
Department of Education
P.O. Box 30008
Lansing, MI 48909
517-373-8425
Fax: 517-335-3630

Minnesota

Adult Basic Education
Department of Education
997 Capital Square Building
550 Cedar Street
St. Paul, MN 55101
612-296-8311
Fax: 612-297-5695

Mississippi

Director of Literacy
State Board for Community and Junior
Colleges
Education and Research Center
3825 Ridgewood Road
Jackson, MS 39211
601-982-6344
Fax: 601-359-2326

Missouri

Director, Adult Education
Department of Elementary and Sec-
ondary Education
P.O. Box 480
Jefferson City, MO 65102
314-751-0887
Fax: 314-751-1179

Montana

Director, Adult Education
State of Public Instruction
Office of the State Superintendent
State Capitol Building
Helena, MT 59602
406-444-4443
Fax: 406-444-3924

Nebraska

Director, Adult and Community
Education
Department of Education
301 Centennial Mall South
P.O. Box 94987
Lincoln, NE 68509
402-471-4807
Fax: 402-471-0117

Nevada

Adult Basic Education Consultant
State GED Administrator
Department of Education
Adult and Continuing Education
400 W. King Street
Capitol Complex
Carson City, NV 89710
702-687-3134
Fax: 702-687-5660

New Hampshire

Supervisor, ABE
Department of Education
101 Pleasant Street
Concord, NH 03301
603-271-6698
Fax: 603-271-1953

New Jersey

Director, A.E.
Department of Education
225 West State Street
Trenton, NJ 08625-0500
609-777-0577
Fax: 609-633-9825

New Mexico

State Director, ABE
Department of Education
Education Building
300 Don Gaspar
Santa Fe, NM 87501
505-827-6672
Fax: 505-827-6696

New York

Director, Division of Continuing
Education
State Education Department
Washington Ave.
Albany, NY 12234
518-474-5808
Fax: 518-474-2801

North Carolina

Director, Continuing Education
Department of Community Colleges
200 West Jones
Raleigh, NC 27063-1337
919-733-4791
Fax: 919-733-0680

North Dakota

Director, Adult Education
Department of Public Instruction
600 Boulevard Avenue East
9th Floor, State Capitol Building
Bismarck, ND 58505-0440
701-224-2393/3600
Fax: 701-224-2461

Ohio

State Director, Adult Education
Department of Education
933 High Street, Suite 210
Worthington, OH 43085-4087
614-466-5015
Fax: 614-752-1640 z9466-2372)

Oklahoma

Director, Lifelong Learning
Department of Education
Oliver Hodge memorial Education
Building
2500 N. Lincoln Blvd., Room 180
Oklahoma City, OK 73105-4599
405-521-3321
Fax: 405-521-6205

Oregon

Office of Assistant Commissioner
Community College Services
255 Capitol St., NE
Salem, OR 97310
503-378-8585
Fax: 503-378-8434

Pennsylvania

Director, Bureau of Adult, Basic and
Literacy Education
Department of Education
333 Market Street, 6th Floor
Harrisburg, PA 17126-0333
717-787-5532
Fax: 717-783-5420

Puerto Rico

Asst. Secretary for Adult Education
Educational Extension
P.O. Box 759
Hato Rey, PR 00919
809-753-9211
Fax: 809-754-0843

Rhode Island

Adult Education Specialist
Department of Education
22 Hayes St., Room 222
Roger Williams Building
Providence, RI 02908
401-277-2705
Fax: 401-277-6033

South Carolina

State Director
Office of Community Education
South Carolina Department of
Education
1429 Senate St.
403 Rutledge Office Building
Columbia, SC 29201
803-734-8563
Fax: 803-734-8624

South Dakota

Adult Education
Office of Adult, Vocational and Technical Education
700 Governors Drive
Pierre, SD 57501-2291
605-773-4716
Fax: 605-773-6139

Tennessee

Executive Director
Division of Adult and Community
Education
Department of Education
1130 Menzler Rd.
Nashville, TN 37210
615-741-7054
Fax: 615-741-6236

Texas

Program Director, Adult Education
Division of A.E./Employment
Training, Funding and Compliance
Texas Education Center
1701 North Congress Avenue
Austin, TX 78701
512-463-9294
Fax: 512-475-3575

Utah

Specialist
Adult Education Services
Office of Education
250 East 500 South St.
Salt Lake City, UT 84111
801-538-7844
Fax: 801-538-7521

Vermont

Chief, Adult Education Unit
Department of Education
State Office Building
Montpelier, VT 05602
802-828-3131
Fax: 802-828-3140

Virginia

Associate Director, A.E.
Department of Education
Commonwealth of Virginia
P.O. Box 6Q
Richmond, VA 23216
804-225-2075
Fax: 804-371-8593

Virgin Islands

Director, ABE
Department of Education
P.O. Box 6640
St. Thomas, VI 00801
809-774-5394
Fax: 809-774-4679

Washington

Director
Office of Adult Literacy
State Board for Community and Technical Colleges
P.O. Box 42495
Olympia, WA 98504-2495
206-664-9402
Fax: 206-664-8808

West Virginia

Assistant Director, A.E.
Department of Education
Building 6, Room 230
Capitol Complex
1900 Kanawha Blvd., East
Charleston, WV 25305
304-558-6318
Fax: 304-558-0048

Wisconsin

State Director, Vocational, Technical and Adult Education
Board of Vocational, Technical and Adult Education
310 Price Place
P.O. Box 7874
Madison, WI 53707
608-266-1207

Wyoming

Coordinator, Adult Education
Hathaway Building
Cheyenne, WY 82002
307-777-6228
Fax: 307-777-6234

State Employment Agencies

The state-by-state lists below will tell you what State Employment Agencies provide career counseling, vocational testing or other special services.

Alabama
Department of Industrial Relations
State Employment Service
649 Monroe Street
Montgomery, AL 36131
334-242-8003
Montgomery local office: 334-286-3700
  Services:
  Career/Vocational Counseling: Yes
  Testing: aptitude
  Other Services and Publications
      — Labor market information
      — Food Stamp Program: job training for individuals on food stamps
      — Professional Placement Services: special counseling and help for white collar professionals

Alaska
Employment Security Division
Department of Labor
P.O. Box 25509
Juneau, AK 99802-5509
Juneau local office: 907-465-2711
> **Services:**
> Career/Vocational Counseling: yes
> Testing: General aptitude, clerical, and self-interest
> Other Services and Publications
> — Alaska Job Facts

Arizona
Department of Economic Security
DES Public Information Office
P.O. Box 6123
1717 W. Jefferson
Phoenix, AZ 85007
602-542-3667
> **Services:**
> Career/Vocational Counseling: yes
> Testing: Aptitude
> Other Services and Publications:
> — Food Stamp/ Job Search: refers eligible job seekers to Food Stamp program
> — Special summer employment campaigns
> — Work Incentive Demonstration Program (Workfare): helps AFDC recipients move toward economic self-support
> — Services Provided by DES

Arkansas
Employment Security Department
#2 Capitol Mall
Little Rock, AR 72203
501-682-2121
Local Little Rock office: 501-682-2127
Services:
Career/Vocational Counseling: only that involving Job Training Partnership Act participants
Testing: yes, aptitude and clerical
Other services and Publications:
  — Labor market information
  — Employer Services: A Good Return on Your Investment; programs that companies use to get the employees they need.

California
Employment Development Department
800 Capitol Mall, Room 5000
Sacramento, CA 95814
916-653-0707
Local Sacramento office: 916-227-0300
Services:
Career/Vocational Counseling: Yes
Testing: Aptitude and clerical
Other Services and Publications:
  — Job Search Workshops
  — Labor market information and statistics
  — Experience Unlimited program—helps unemployed managers, professionals and technical workers get back to work
  — Job Match—computerized service that matches job applicant's skills with state-wide listing of job openings.

Colorado

Department of Labor and Employment
Division of Employment and Training
639 E. 18th Avenue
Denver, CO 80203
303-830-3011

Services:

Career/Vocational Counseling: Yes
Testing: Aptitude
Other Services and Publications:

— Labor market information
— Job Search Workshops-subjects include interviewing, writing resumes and where to look for jobs.
— Forty Plus of Colorado, Inc.—organizations of unemployed people 40 years of age or older who have professional or management experience and who help each other with job search.
— Summer Job Hunt—helps kids ages 16 through 21 find summer jobs.
— Year-round Youth Program—kids receive job placement help.
— Stay In School Campaign—kids who need money to stay in school can get certified to work part-time in the summer for the federal government.

Connecticut
Connecticut Department of Labor
Program Support
200 Folly Brook Blvd.
Wethersfield, CT 06109-1114
203-566-5160
Hartford local office: 203-566-5771
> **Services:**
> Career/Vocational Counseling: Yes
> Testing: Clerical, Aptitude, Interest
> Other Services and Publications:
> > — Shared Work Program: part-time employment along with proportional unemployment benefits
> > — Job Connection: businesses get tax credit for providing on-the-job training.
> > — Customized Job Training: group of workers are trained for a specific business's needs.
> > — Subsidized Transitional Employment Program: companies get wage subsidies as an incentive to hire certain workers.
> > — Employment Search Program: job help for mothers on welfare
> > — Labor market information.

Delaware
Department of Labor
Employment and Training Division
P.O. Box 9499
Newark, DE 19714-9499
302-761-8129
Newark local office: 302-368-6622
> **Services:**
> Career/Vocational Counseling: Yes
> Testing: Aptitude
> Other Services and Publications
> > — Directory of Job Training, Employment & Education Programs: includes listing of organizations and agencies in DE that offer job training programs.
> > — Women's Vocational Services: special employment and training services for divorced or separated women.

District of Columbia

Office of Job Service
Department of Employer Services
500 C St., NW, Room 317
Washington, DC 20001
202-724-7049

Services:

Career/Vocational Counseling: Yes
Testing: Clerical and Aptitude
Other Services and Publications:

— First Source Agreement Program: certain D.C. contractors must give job preference to D.C. residents

— Regional Employment Program: matches D.C. workers with job openings in the MD and VA suburbs

— A Real Chance: job opportunities for public assistance recipients

— Adult Literacy programs

— On-the-job training companies receive financial incentives to provide workers with on-the-job training.

— Training and Retraining for Employment Program: referrals, job placement, training, and allowances for those needing training.

Florida

Department of Labor and Employment Security
1320 Executive Center Dr.
300 Atkins Building
Tallahassee, FL 32301
904-488-7228

Services:

Career/Vocational Counseling: Yes, including workshops
Testing: Clerical and Aptitude
Other Services and Publications:

— Professional Placement Network: helps unemployed professionals find work through networking.

— Job Club: activities include resume writing, interviewing techniques, and more

— Job Skills Workshop

Georgia
Employment Services Division
Department of Labor
148 International Blvd.
Atlanta, GA 30303
404-656-6380
Atlanta local office: 404-699-6900
Services:
Career/Vocational Counseling: No
Testing: Clerical
Other Services and Publications:
- (Re)Place Yourself: A Job Hunting Guide
- Personal Data Book: A Record for Job Hunters
- Job Corps Services: screening for applicants
- OLIVOR System: a computerized system for unemployment benefits.

Hawaii
Hawaii State Employment Service
830 Punch Bowl St., Room 112
Honolulu, HI 96813
808-586-8700
Services:
Career/Vocational Counseling: On a very limited basis as time permits for general applicant. Do provide Veterans counseling.
Testing: No
For JTPA contact: Work Hawaii Brochure, 715 South King St., Suite 500, Honolulu, Hawaii 96813, 808-523-4221.
- Referral to job training programs
- Improving your English—referrals to free English improvement programs
- Child care and transportation—will help you with free transportation or child care if you need it while job searching.
- Disabled Veterans Outreach Program—helps veterans directly in their job search.

Idaho
Idaho Department of Employment
317 Main Street
Boise, ID 83735
208-334-6100
Boise local office: 208-334-6211
> **Services:**
> Career/Vocational Counseling: Yes
> Testing: Clerical and Aptitude
> Other Services and Publications:
>> — Rent-A-Kid Program: Job Service calls daily on kids to fill positions for employers.
>> — Wage Surveys for irrigators

Illinois
Department of Employment Security
401 S. State Street
Chicago, IL 60605
312-793-5700
Aurora local Job Service office: 708-844-6640
> **Services:**
> Career/Vocational Counseling: Yes, with emphasis on Vets
> Testing: Clerical and Job Skills Aptitude
> Other Services and Publications:
>> — Hire The Future: summer job program for teens
>> — Job Search computer system: matches applicants with job openings.
>> — Job Search Workshops
>> — Doorways to Jobs: A Directory of Job Training
>> — Illinois Department of Employment Security Services
>> — Merchandising Your Job Talents.

Indiana
Department of Workforce Development
10 N. Senate
Indianapolis, IN 46204
317-232-7670
Local Indianapolis office: 317-6842400
Services:
Career/Vocational Counseling: Yes, through workshops
Testing: Yes, guidance testing and referral
Other Services and Publications:
- Basic Education Classes
- Training Opportunities Workshops
- On-the-Job Training
- Academic Skills Upgrades: conducts classes for companies whose workers need to be better educated.
- Industry-Based Training: pays companies to retrain workers in-house.
- Labor market information

Iowa
Job Service Program Bureau
Department of Employment Services
1000 East Grand Avenue
Des Moines, IA 50319
800-562-4692
Des Moines local office: 512-281-9619
Services:
Career/Vocational Counseling: Yes
Testing: Clerical

Kansas

Division of Employment and Training
Department of Human Resources
401 Topeka Avenue
913-296-5317

Services:
Career/Vocational Counseling: Yes
Testing: Aptitude, Clerical
Other Services and Publications:
Job Search Workshops
Chamber of Commerce relocation package: 913-234-2644
Career Assistance Network: 913-273-5190
Topeka Youth Project: 913-273-4141

Kentucky

Department of Employment Services
275 East Main Street, 2nd Floor
Frankfort, KY 40621
502-564-5331
Local Office: 502-564-7046 (Frankfort)

Services:
Career/Vocational Counseling: Yes
Testing: Occupational, Clerical, Aptitude, Toyota Motor Corporation Skills Testing
Other Services and Publications:

— On-the-job training

— JOBS: Job training and placement program for AFDC recipients.

— Professional Placement Network: help for management-level professionals who have lost their jobs—502-564-3906.

Louisiana
Office of Employment Security
Department of Labor
P.O. Box 94094
Baton Rouge, LA 70804-9094
504-342-3013
Local Baton Rouge office: 504-925-4311
Services:
Career/Vocational Counseling: No
Testing: Aptitude, Clerical
Other Services and Publications:
— Labor Market Information
— On-the-job Training
— Shared Work Unemployment Compensation: workers can work part-time and still earn a proportion of the unemployment insurance.

Maine
Job Service Division
Bureau of Employment Security
P.O. Box 309
Augusta, ME 04330
207-287-3431
Local Augusta office: 207-624-5120
Services:
Career/Vocational Counseling: Yes
Testing: General Aptitude
Other Services and Publications:
— Strategic Training for Accelerated Reemployment Program: help for those on unemployment get the help and training they need.
— Health Occupations Training Project: education and training in health care jobs.
— Jobs for Maine's Graduates Program: helps high school students make transition from school to job market.
— Maine Training Initiative Program: job training for those who don't qualify for JTPA job training.
— Summer Youth Program: provides work and basic education for teens during the summer.
— Resume Preparation Assistance.

Maryland

Job Service
Department of Employment and Economic Development
1100 North Eutaw St., Room 208
Baltimore, MD 21201
410-767-2000
Local Baltimore office: 410-767-2121

Services:
Career/Vocational Testing: Yes
Testing: Clerical, Aptitude
Other Services and Publications:
On-the-job Training
Courses offered at local community college
Area skill development centers

Massachusetts

Department of Employment and Training
19 Staniford Street
Boston, MA 02114
617-626-6000
Boston local office: 617-626-6000

Services:
Career/Vocational counseling Yes, job specialists available
Testing: Clerical, Aptitude
Other Services and Publications:

— Training and Employment Directory: listing of jobs and places to get the necessary training for them in the state.
— Personal employment plan: creates a special job plant to your needs.
— Resume writing services
— Job search workshops

Use of:
Fax machines
Photocopiers
Telephones
Job guides
Labor market books
Career resource materials
Child care listings
Transportation information

Michigan
Bureau of Employment Service
Employment Security Commission
7310 Woodward Ave.
Detroit, MI 48202
313-876-5309
Local Detroit office: 313-822-9510
Services:
Career/Vocational Counseling: Yes
Testing: Aptitude, Clerical, Interest Inventory
Other Services and Publications:
Labor market data
Local statewide, and interstate job banks
Job service resume system
Job development
Job seeking skills workshops and Job Clubs
Occupational information

Minnesota
Reemployment Program
Administration
390 N. Roberts St.
St. Paul, MN 55101
612-297-2177
Local St. Paul office: 612-642-0363
Services:
Career/Vocational Counseling: Yes, to those facing employment barriers
Testing: Proficiency and aptitude as well as vocational
Other Services and Publications:
— Mass recruitment: screening for companies needing large numbers of workers.
— Referral to community-based agencies

Mississippi

Mississippi Employment Security Commission
1520 West Capitol Street
P.O. Box 1699
Jackson, MS 39215-1699
601-961-7478
601-354-8711
Southfort local office: 601-961-7802

Services:

Career/Vocational Counseling: Yes
Testing: Yes, Clerical, Aptitude (not all offices)
Other Services and Publications:
— Labor market Information

Missouri

Employment Services
Division of Employment Security (DOLIR)
P.O. Box 59
Jefferson City, MO 65104
314-751-3976
Jefferson local office: 314-526-8115

Services:

Career/Vocational Counseling: Yes
Testing: Clerical, when requested by employer
Other Services and Publications:
— Automated job match: your skills, abilities and salary requirements are matched up with available job openings.
— Missouri Resume Retrieval Service: when job opening occurs, your resume automatically sent to employer.
— Labor Market Information.

Montana
Job Service/Employment and Training Division
P.O. Box 1728
Helena, MT 59624
406-444-4100
Helena local office: 406-447-3200
Services:
Career/Vocational Counseling: Yes
Testing: Aptitude, Clerical, Literacy, Interest
Other Services and Publications:
- — Teacher Placement: special program that matches up teachers and school administrators with available job openings in MT.
- — On-the-job training: businesses received subsidy to provide workers with on-the-job training.
- — For A Working Montana: outlines all the job programs
- — Job matching system
- — Labor market information

Nebraska
Job Training Program
Department of Labor
P.O. Box 94600
Lincoln, NE 68509
402-471-2127
Lincoln local office: 402-441-7111
Services:
Career/Vocational Counseling: Yes
Testing: Aptitude
Other Services and Publications:
- — Work Experience: a paid employment experience with a public or non-profit agency.
- — Classroom training: available through community colleges.
- — Pacific Institute: develops independent thinking skills to set personal and professional goals.
- — On-the-Job training.

Nevada

Department of Employment, Training, and Rehabilitation
Employment Security Division
500 East Third Street
Carson City, NV 89713
702-687-4650
Carson City local office: 702-687-4560
Services:
Vocational/Career Counseling: Yes
Testing: Aptitude, Performance, Interest
Other Services and Publications:
> On-the-job Training
> Claimant Employment Program: helps put workers claiming unemployment into job training programs.
> Job Search Skills Workshops: resume preparation, interviewing skills, and appropriate dress.
> Short-term Labor: provides part-time work for those eligible to work at a moment's notice.
> Employment Guide: Nevada Job Finding Techniques.

New Hampshire

Employment Service Bureau
Department of Employment Security
32 South Main Street
Concord, NH 03301
603-224-3311
Local Concord Office: 603-228-4100
Services:
Vocational/Career Counseling: Yes
Testing: Aptitude, Performance, Interest
Other Services and Publications:
> Outstanding Personnel List: local employment offices select job seekers who have high levels of achievement to show employers.
> Community Work Experience Program: gain work experience through community organizations.
> On-the-job training.
> Referral to supportive services.
> How to Prepare Yourself for Job Interviews
> Veterans Resource Directory
> Job Interviewing Techniques

New Jersey

Employment Services
New Jersey Department of Labor
Labor and Industry Bldg., CN 058
Trenton, NJ 08625
609-292-5005
Local Office: 609-292-0620

Services:

Career/Vocational Counseling: Yes
Testing: GATB, Uses Interest Inventory
— Vocational Information Profile (VIP)
Other Services and Publications:
— Career evaluation
— Training programs for newly locating companies: companies new to an area and looking for skilled workers may qualify for free training.
— Job Development
— World of Work seminars
— Job Hunters Guide

New Mexico

New Mexico Department of Labor
P.O. Box 1928
Albuquerque, NM 87103
505-841-8406
Local Office: 505-841-9327

Services:

Career/Vocational Counseling
Testing: Clerical, Aptitude
Other Services and Publications:
— Career Information System: computer program that tells you what you need to do given your background and career goals.
— Large Employers in the Albuquerque Area

New York

New York State Department of Labor
Community Service Division
State Campus
Building 12, Room 582
Albany, NY 12240
518-457-3584
Local Office: 518-465-0797

Services:
Career/Vocational Counseling: Yes
Testing: Aptitude, clerical, literacy and career interest
Other Services and Publications:

— On-the-job training: screen workers for available opportunities to train on the job.
— Displaced Homemaker Program: provides counseling, training, support services and job placement to homemakers who have lost their support.
— Job Search Skills: tip sheets, workshops, and seminars
— Project Trabago: makes sure job programs are accessible to Hispanic community; provides needed translation help.
— Rural Programs: offer help to seasonal farm workers find jobs.
— Community services: referral to appropriate human service programs for the unemployed.
— Benefits for Veterans and Their Families.

North Carolina

Employment Security Commission
P.O. Box 27625
Raleigh, NC 27611
919-733-7522
Local office: 919-733-3941

Services:
Vocational/Career Counseling: Yes
Testing: Aptitude, Clerical

North Dakota
Employment and Training Division
Job Service
P.O. Box 5507
Bismarck, ND 58502
701-328-2861
Loval Job Service: 701-328-5000
Services:
Vocational/Career Counseling: Yes
Testing: Aptitude and Interest, Typing and Spelling
Other Services and Publications:
Job Search Assistance workshops
JOBS

Ohio
Ohio Employment Service Division
Ohio Bureau of Employment Services
145 South Front Street
Columbus, OH 43215
614-466-4636
Local office: 614-268-7990 (North)
614-237-2585 (East)
Services:
Vocational/Career Counseling: Yes
Testing: Clerical, Aptitude
Other Services and Publications:
- — Child care information: provides a computer printout of licensed day care centers in your area.
- — Ex-offender services
- — Writing an Effective Resume
- — Job Search Techniques
- — Ohio Military Transition Assistance Program
- — Job Search Strategies

Oklahoma

Oklahoma Employment Service
Employment Security Commission
Will Rogers Memorial Office Building
2401 North Lincoln Blvd.
Oklahoma City, OK 73105
405-557-0200
Local office: 405-424-0881
Services:
Vocational/Career Counseling: Yes
Testing: Spelling, Typing and Dictation
Other Services and Publications:
- — Labor market information
- — Job Development: Service contacts employer on behalf of job applicant with specific skills where no job openings in the local office for that particular skill.
- — Computerized Matching: job seekers are matched with job openings.

Oregon

Oregon Employment Department
875 Union Street, NE
Salem, OR 97311
503-378-8420
Local Office: 503-378-4846
Services:
Vocational/Career Counseling: only through the JTPA program
Testing: Clerical (nonaptitude available)
Other Services and Publications:
- — Timber Industry Dislocated Workers Program

Pennsylvania
Bureau of Job Center Field Operations
Labor and Industry Building, Room 419
Seventh and Forster Streets
Harrisburg, PA 17121
717-787-3354
Local Office: 717-783-3270
Services:
Vocational/Career Counseling: Yes
Testing: Skills Testing: Aptitude (when requested by employer)
Other Services and Publications:
Pennsylvania Conservation Corps: summer and year-round work on public
land and in community centers for young people, ages 14 to 25.
On-the-Job Training
Career Guide Newspaper

Rhode Island
Department of Employment and Training
101 Friendship Street
Providence, RI 02903
401-277-3732
Local Office: 401-277-3606
Services:
Vocational/Career Counseling: Yes
Testing: GATB, CDM (Career Decision Maker) and APTICOM, as
well as clerical
Other Services and Publications:
— Job Search Workshops: covers interviewing,
  applications, and marketing job skills
— Resume Writing Seminars: professionally printed
  resumes provided to help you with job search.
— Call-A-Teen Program: a statewide, odd job employment
  programs for teens 14 to 17 years old.
— Tuition Waivers: for courses at state colleges or
  universities if you're receiving benefits.

South Carolina
South Carolina Employment Service
P.O. Box 995
Columbia, SC 29202
803-737-2400
Local Office: 803-737-9935
Services:
Vocational/Career Counseling: Yes
Testing: Clerical, at employers request, aptitude
Other Services and Publications:
— Rural manpower service programs: help seasonal farmworkers with referrals to employment agencies and support services.
— South Carolina Employer Services Catalog.

South Dakota
South Dakota Department of Labor
700 Governors Drive
Pierre, SD 57501
605-773-3101
Local Office: 605-773-3372
Services:
Vocational/Career Counseling: yes
Testing: yes, clerical aptitude
Other Services and Publications:
— Job Related Education: job specific education that furthers the training in your chosen field.
— Skill Training: training conducted for up to two years at vocational schools and college.
— Work Experience program: pays you federal minimum wage while you work at a real job.
— How Job Service Can Help You Find A Job
— How Job Training Can Improve Your Work Skills

Tennessee
Department of Employment Security
Volunteer Plaza, 12th Floor
500 James Robertson Parkway
Nashville, TN 37243
615-741-2131
Local Office: 615-741-3626
Services:
Vocational/Career Counseling: yes
Testing: Aptitude
Other Services and Publications:
— Referral to skill training

Texas
Texas Employment Commission
101 East 15th Street
Austin, TX 78778
512-463-2222
Local Office: 512-478-8734
Information: 512-463-2873
Services:
Other Services and Publications:
— Annual Report of the Texas Employment Commission

Utah
Job Service
Department of Employment Security
Administration
140 East, 300 South
Salt Lake City, UT 84101
801-536-7400
Public Relations: 801-536-7462
Local Office: 801-536-7000
Services:
Vocational/Career Counseling: yes
Testing: GATB, Proficiency (typing, dictation, spelling)
Other Services and Publications:
Temporary Placement Offices in Salt Lake and Ogden
Job Seeking Skills Workshop
Labor market information

Vermont

Employment Service Administration
Department of Employment and Training
P.O. Box 488
Montpelier, VT 05602
802-229-0311
Local Office: 802-828-3860

Services:

Vocational/Career Counseling: yes
Testing: GATB, Interest Inventory Profile (VIP), Basic Skills assessments
Other Services and Publications:

— Group Assessment (COMPASS): help in focusing on career choices.

— Vermont Occupational Information System: information on job projections, job specific education.

— Federal Occupational and Career Information System: matches your interests and abilities with suitable Federal jobs.

— State Training Inventory: a computer file of training programs being offered at schools and training institutions in the northeast.

Virginia

Virginia Employment Commissioner
703 East Main Street
Richmond, VA 23219
804-786-3001
Local office: 804-674-3650

Services:

Career/Vocational Counseling: yes
Testing: Typing, if required by job order
Other Services and Publications:

— JOBS program: offers education, training, and job-related services to welfare recipients.

— Federal Contractor Job Listing: companies with large federal government contracts lists jobs with VA Job Service.

— Labor market information

— Employability training

Washington

Washington Employment Security Department
TRB 2 Unit
P.O. Box 9046
Olympia, WA 98507-9046
360-753-0747
Local Office: 206-438-7800

Services:

Career/Vocational Counseling: yes
Testing: Not on a regular basis, although will do some aptitude testing for specific individuals with need
Other Services and Publications:

— JobNet: matches workers' skills and abilities with available jobs in any geographical area.
— Classroom, vocational and on-the-job training
— Job Search Workshops: resume writing, interviewing techniques, grooming and more.
— Job Search Skills Training Program: special retraining program for workers who have been injured on the job.
— Special Employment Services (Dislocated Timber Workers): screens unemployed timber workers who are eligible to receive four days of work and one day of training per week.

West Virginia

West Virginia Bureau of Employment Programs
112 California Ave.
Charleston, WV 25305-0112
304-558-2630
Local Office: 304-558-0342

Services:

Career/Vocational Counseling: yes
Testing: Aptitude and proficiency tests
Other Services and Publications:

Wisconsin
Department of DILHR
Job Service, 2nd Florr
201 East Washington Ave.
Madison, WI 53702
608266-0327 Department of Job Service
Local office: 608-266-1492
Services:
Vocational/Career counseling: Yes
Testing: Typing, general aptitude (for apprenticeships only)
Other Services and Publications:
Setting Employment Goals
Interviewing Skills/Techniques
Resume and Job Search Assistance

Wyoming
Wyoming Department of Employment
P.O. Box 2760
Casper, WY 82602
307-235-3611
Services:
Career/Vocational Counseling: Yes
Testing and Assessment Services: Yes
Other Services:
Computerized listing of job openings
On-the-job training
Labor market information
Resume preparation assistance
Workshops
Resource center

U.S. Office of Personnel Management

Federal Employment Information Centers

Alabama
520 Wynn Drive N.W.
Huntsville, AL 35818-3426
205-837-0894

Alaska
222 West 7th Ave., #22 Room 158
Anchorage, AK 99513-7522
907-271-5821

Arizona
(See New Mexico)

California
9650 Flair Dr., Suite 100A
El Monte, CA 91731
818-575-6510

1029 J St., Room 202
Sacramento, CA 95814
416-744-5627

Federal Building, Room 4260
880 Front Street
San Diego, CA 92101
818-575-8510
120 Howard Street, Suite B
San Francisco, CA 94120
415-744-5627

Colorado
12345 W. Alameda Parkway
Lakewood, CO 60225
303-969-7050

Connecticut
(See Boston, Massachusetts)

Delaware
(See Philadelphia, Pennsylvania)

District of Columbia
Theodore Roosevelt Federal Building
1900 E St., NW, Room 1416
Washington, DC 20415
202-606-2700

Florida
Claude Pepper Federal Building,
Room 1222
61 SW First Avenue
Miami, FL (walk in only)

Commodore Building, Suite 125
3444 McCrory Place
Orlando, FL (walk in only)

Georgia
Richard B. Russell Building, Room 940A
75 Spring Street, SW
Atlanta, GA 30303
404-331-4315

Hawaii
Federal Building, Room 5316
300 Alamoana Blvd.
Honolulu, HI 96850
808-541-2791

Idaho
(See Seattle, Washington)

Illinois
230 South Dearborn St., Room 2916
Chicago, IL 60804
312-353-6192

Indiana
(See Michigan)

Iowa
(See Kansas City, Missouri)
816-426-7820

Kentucky
(See Ohio)

Louisiana
1515 Poydras St., Suite 608
New Orleans, LA 70112
210-805-2402

Maine
(See Philadelphia, Pennsylvania)

Massachusetts
10 Causeway Street
Boston, MA 02222
617-565-5900

Michigan
477 Michigan Avenue, Room 565
Detroit, MI 48228
313-226-6950

Minnesota
Bishop Henry Whipple Federal Bldg.
1 Federal Drive, Room 501
Fort Snelling, MN 55111
612-725-3430

Mississippi
(See Alabama)

Missouri
Federal Building, Room 134
601 E. 12th Street
Kansas City, MO 64106
816-426-5702

400 Old Post Office Building
815 Olive Street
St. Louis, MO 63101
314-539-2285

Montana
(See Colorado)

Nebraska
(See Kansas City)
816-426-7819

Nevada
(for Clark, Lincoln, and Nye counties,
see Los Angeles, California: all other
counties See Sacramento, California)

New Hampshire
(See Boston, Massachusetts)

New Jersey
(See New York City, New York
or Philadelphia, Pennsylvania)

New Mexico
605 Marquette Avenue, Suite 910
Albuquerque, NM 87102
505-766-5583

New York
Jacob K. Javits Building
Second Floor, Room 120
26 Federal Plaza
New York City, NY 10278
212-264-0422

P.O. Box 7267
100 South Clinton Street
Syracuse, NY 13261
315-448-0480

North Carolina
4407 Bland Road, Suite 202
Raleigh, NC 27609
919-790-2822

North Dakota
(See Minnesota)

Ohio
Federal Building, Room 506
200 W. 2nd Street
Dayton, OH 45402
513-225-2720

Oklahoma
(See San Antonio, Texas)

Oregon
Federal Building, Room 376
1220 SW Third Ave.
Portland, OR 97204
503-326-3141

Pennsylvania
Federal Building, Room 168
P.O. Box 761
Harrisburg, PA 17108
717-782-4494

William J. Green, Jr. Federal Building
600 Arch Street
Philadelphia, PA 19106
215-597-7440

Federal Building
1000 Liberty Ave., Room 119
Pittsburgh, PA 15222
(See Philadelphia for telephone)

Puerto Rico
U.S. Federal Building, Room 328
150 Carlos Chardon Avenue
San Juan, PR 00918
609-766-5242

Rhode Island
(See Boston, Massachusetts)

South Carolina
(See Raleigh, North Carolina)

South Dakota
(See Minnesota)

Tennessee
(See Alabama)

Texas
(Corpus Christi: see San Antonio)
512-884-8113

Dallas
(See San Antonio)

Harlingen
(See San Antonio)
512-769-0455

8610 Broadway, Room 305
San Antonio, TX 78217
210-805-2402

Utah
(See Colorado)

Vermont
(See Puerto Rico)
809-774-8790

Virginia
Federal Building, Room 500
200 Granby Street
Norfolk, VA 23510
804-441-3335

Washington
Federal Building, Room 110
915 Second Avenue
Seattle, WA 98174
206-220-6400

Washington, DC
(See District of Columbia)

West Virginia
(See Ohio)
513-225-2866

Wisconsin
(for Dane, Grant, Green, Iowa, Lafayette,
Jefferson, Walworth, Milwaukee, Racine,

Waukesha, Rock and Kenosha, see Illinois listing. 312-353-6189; for all Other counties see Minnesota, 612-725-3430)

Wyoming
(See Colorado)

State Government Jobs

Be certain to complete in detail the job application and file it with the designated before the deadline date. If you are a veteran you will undoubtedly get a preference. Also note whether a written examination is required for the job.

Alabama
State Personnel Department
300 State Administration Building
64 North Union Street
Montgomery, AL 36130
334-242-3389

Alaska
Alaska Division of Personnel
Department of Administration
P.O. Box 110201
Juneau, AK 99811-0201
907-465-4430
Job Bank: 907-465-8910
www.state.ak.us

Arizona
Arizona State Personnel Division
Department of Administration
1831 W. Jefferson
Phoenix, AZ 85007
602-542-5482
Job Bank: 602-542-4966
www.state.az.us

Arkansas
Office of Personnel Management
Department of Finance and
Administration
1509 W. 7th St., Room 201
Little Rock, AR 72201
501-682-1823
Job Bank: 501-682-5627
www.state.ar.us

California
California State Personnel
P.O. Box 944201
Sacramento, CA 94244-2010
916-653-1705
Los Angeles: 213-620-6450
San Diego: 619-237-6163
San Francisco: 415-557-7871
TDD: 916-445-2689
Job Bank: 916-445-0538
www.ca.gov

Colorado
State Dept. of Human Resources
1313 Sherman Street, Room 110
Denver, CO 80203
303-866-2321
www.state.co.us

Connecticut
State Resource and Employment Center
165 Capitol Avenue
Hartford, CT 06106
203-566-2501
www.state.ct.us

Delaware
State Personnel Office
First Street Plaza, 3rd Floor
Wilmington, DE 19801
302-739-4195
www.state.de.us

District of Columbia
D.C. Personnel Department
441 4th Street, NW
Washington, DC 20001
202-727-6099
www.dchomepage.net

Florida
State Personnel Department
Room 1902
The Capitol
Tallahassee, FL 32399-0250
904-488-1176
Job Bank: 904-488-1179
Fax: 904-922-4928
www.state.fl.us

Georgia
Merit System of Personnel Admin.
West Tower, Suite 418
200 Piedmont Avenue
Atlanta, GA 30334
404-656-2705
Job Bank: 404-656-2725
Fax: 404-656-9740

Hawaii
Hawaii Department of Personnel
235 South Beretania Street, 11th Fl.
Honolulu, HA 96813-2437
808-587-0977
Job Bank: 808-587-0977
Fax: 808-587-1003
www.state.hawaii.gov

Idaho
State Personnel Commission
P.O. Box 83720
Boise, ID 83720-0066
208-334-2263
800-554-JOBS
Job Bank: 208-334-2568
Fax: 208-334-3182
www.state.id.us

Illinois
Bureau of Personnel Department of
Management Services
503 Stratton Office Building
Springfield, IL 62706
217-782-6179
Fax: 217-524-8740
www.state.il.us

Indiana
Indiana Department of Personnel
402 West Washington St.
Indiana Government Center South
Indianapolis, IN 46204-2261
317-232-3105
Fax: 317-233-0236
www.state.in.us./acin/personnel

Iowa
Iowa Department of Personnel
Grimes State Office Building
East 14th and Grand
Des Moines, IA 50319
515-281-3351
Fax: 515-242-6450
Job Bank: 515-281-5820
www.state.ia.us/jobs/index.htm

Kansas

Kansas Division of Personnel Services
Department of Administration
Room 951, South Landon Building
Topeka, KS 66612
913-296-5390
www.state.ks.us

Kentucky

Kentucky Department of Personnel
200 Fair Oaks Lane, Suite 517
Frankfort, KY 40601
502-564-4460
www.state.ky.us

Louisiana

Louisiana Civil Service Commission
Division of Personnel
P.O. box 94111
Baton Rouge, LA 70804-9111
504-342-8536
Fax: 504-342-2386
www.state.la.us

Maine

Human Resources Department
4 Statehouse
Augusta, ME 04333
207-287-3761
www.state.me.us

Maryland

Maryland Department of Personnel
301 West Preston Street
Baltimore, MD 21201
410-225-4851
Fax: 410-333-5764
http://dop.state.md.us

Massachusetts

Division of Personnel Administration
1 Ashburton Place
Boston, MA 02108
617-727-3777
Fax: 617-727-3970
www.magnet.state.ma.us

Michigan

Michigan Department of Civil
Services
400 South Pine
P.O. Box 30002
Lansing, MI 48909
517-373-2819
Fax: 517-373-7690

Minnesota

Minnesota Department of Employee
Relations
200 Centennial Office Building
658 Cedar Street
St. Paul, MN 55155
612-296-8366
Fax: 612-296-8919
www.state.mn.us

Mississippi

Mississippi State Personnel Board
301 North Lamar Street, Suite 100
Jackson, MS 39201
601-359-2725
Fax: 601-359-2380
www.state.ms.us

Missouri

Missouri Division of Personnel
P.O. Box 388
Jefferson City, MO 65102
314-751-4162
Fax: 573-751-8641
www.state.mo.us

Montana

Montana Personnel Division
Mitchell Building, Room 130
Helena, MT 59620
406-444-3871
Fax: 406-447-3224
www.mt.gov

Nebraska

Nebraska Department of Personnel
301 Centennial Mall South
P.O. Box 94905
Lincoln, NE 68509
402-471-2075
Job Bank: 402-471-2200
Fax: 407-471-3754
www.state.ne.us

Nevada

Nevada Department of Personnel
209 East Musser St.
Carson City, NV 89710
702-687-4050
Job Bank: 702-687-4160

New Hampshire

New Hampshire Div. of Personnel
25 Capitol St., Room 1
Concord, NH 03301
603-271-3261
www.state.nh.us

New Jersey

New Jersey Department of Personnel
44 South Clinton Avenue, CN318
Trenton, NJ 08625
609-292-8668
Fax: 609-777-0905
www.state.nj.us

New Mexico

New Mexico State Personnel Office
P.O. Box 26127
Santa Fe, NM 87502-0127
www.state.nm.us

New York

New York State Personnel Board
Department of Civil Services
State Campus, Building #1
Albany, NY 12239
518-457-6216
518-457-3701
www.state.ny.us

North Carolina

North Carolina Office of State
Personnel
116 West Jones St.
Raleigh, NC 27603
919-733-7922
Fax: 919-733-0653
www.state.nc.us

North Dakota

North Dakota Central Personnel
Division
Office of Management and Budget
State Capitol
600 East Blvd., Avenue
Bismarck, ND 58505
701-328-3290
Fax: 701-328-5049
www.state.nd.us

Ohio

Ohio Division of Personnel
Division of Human Resources
30 East Broad St., 28th Floor
Columbus, OH 43215
614-466-4026
Job Bank: 614-466-4026
www.ohio.gov

Oklahoma

Office of Personnel Management
Jim Thorpe Building, Room 22
Oklahoma City, OK 73105
405-521-6337
Fax: 405-521-6308

Oregon

Oregon Personnel and Labor Relations Division
155 Cottage St., NE
Salem, OR 97310
503-378-5419
www.state.or.us

Pennsylvania
Pennsylvania State Employment
Services
Office of Administration
110 Finance Building
Harrisburg, PA 17120
717-787-5703
www.state.pa.us

Rhode Island
Office of Personnel Administration
Department of Administration
One Capitol Hill
Providence, RI 02908
401-277-2172
Fax: 401-277-6391

South Carolina
South Carolina Human Resources
Management Division
221 Divine St., 1st Floor
Columbus, SC 29250
803-734-9333
Fax: 803-734-9098
www.state.sc.us

South Dakota
South Dakota Office of Executive
Management
Bureau of Personnel
500 East Capitol Avenue
Pierre, SD 57501
605-773-4918
Job Bank: 605-773-3326
Fax: 605-773-4344
www.state.sd.us

Tennessee
Tennessee Department of Personnel
James K. Polk Building, 2nd Floor
500 Deadrick Street
Nashville, TN 37243
615-741-4841
Fax: 615-741-6985
www.state.tn.us

Texas
Texas State Employment Commission
101 East 15th Street
Austin, TX 78778
512-463-1792
www.texas.gov

Utah
Utah Department of Human
Resources Management
2120 State Office Building
Salt Lake City, UT 84114
801-538-3058
Job Bank: 801-538-3118
Fax: 801-538-3081
www.state.ut.us

Vermont
Vermont Department of Personnel
110 State Street
Montpelier, VT 05602
802-828-3483
Job Bank: 802-828-3483
Fax: 802-828-3409
www.vermont.state

Virginia
Virginia Department of Personnel and
Training
James Monroe Building, 12th Floor
101 North 14th Street
Richmond, VA 23219
804-225-2131
Fax: 804-371-7401
www.state.va.us

Washington
Washington Department of Personnel
521 Capitol Way South
P.O. Box 47500
Olympia, WA 98504-7500
360-753-5358
Job Bank: 360-753-586-0545
www.wa.gov

West Virginia
West Virginia Division of Personnel
Capitol Complex Building, #6,
Rm. 416
1900 Kanawha Blvd.
Charleston, WV 25305
304-558-5946
Fax: 304-558-1399
www.state.wv.us

Wisconsin
Wisconsin Department of Employ-
ment Relations
137 East Wilson Street
P.O. Box 7855
Madison, WI 53707-7855
608-266-9820
Job Bank: 608-266-1731
Fax: 608-267-1000
www.state.wi.us

Wyoming
Wyoming Personnel Division
Department of Administration and
Information
2001 Capitol Av., Emerson Building
Cheyenne, WY 82002
307-777-6713
www.state.wy.us

About Amber Classics

Amber Classics is a new imprint of Amber Communications Group, Inc., the nation's largest African-American publisher of Self-Help Books and Music Biographies.

Amber Classics will consist of a complete itinerary of reference guides that give African Americans the tools they need to accomplish their specific goals. The Catalog will include information about such topics as: Scholarships, Employment, Real Estate, Self-Publishing, Financial Planning, Legal Information, Teen Advice, Entertainment, Fashion, Beauty, Hair Care, and more.

With the launching of *Amber Classics*, Amber Communications Group, Inc. plans to enter a new niche market that provides readers with the specific information they need without adding excessive dialogue that is not relevant to their goals. The Trade Paperback book reference collection will also be available as very affordable eBooks at prices starting as low as 99 cents.

ACGI's other imprints include: the award winning Amber Books Publishing; Colossus Books - Music Biographies; Amber/Wiley Books - Self Help and Financial Books Co-Published with John Wiley & Sons Inc. and Joyner/Amber Books - Co-Publishing with the Tom Joyner Foundation.

For further information, email: amberbk@aol.com or call: 602-743-7211. Visit: WWW.AMBERBOOKS.COM.

ORDER FORM

WWW.AMBERBOOKS.COM
African-American Self Help and Career Guide Books

Fax Orders: 480-283-0991

Telephone Orders: 602-743-7211
Online Orders: E-mail: amberbk@aol.com

Postal Orders: Send Checks & Money Orders to:
Amber Books Publishing
1334 E. Chandler Blvd., Suite 5-D67
Phoenix, AZ 85048

_____ *The African American Employment Guide*, $14.95

_____ *The African American Scholarship Guide*, $14.95

Name:_____

Company Name:_____

Address:_____

City:_____State:___Zip:_____

Telephone: (____) _____E-mail:_____

For Bulk Rates Call: **602-743-7211**   **ORDER NOW**

Scholarship Guide $14.95
Employment Guide $14.95

❑ Check ❑ Money Order ❑ Cashiers Check
❑ Credit Card: ❑ MC ❑ Visa ❑ Amex ❑ Discover

CC#_____

Expiration Date:_____

Payable to:
   Amber Books
   1334 E. Chandler Blvd., Suite 5-D67
   Phoenix, AZ 85048

Shipping: $5.00 per book. Allow 7 days for delivery.
Sales Tax: Add 8.3% to books shipped to Arizona addresses.

Total enclosed: $_____

CPSIA information can be obtained at www.ICGtesting.com
Printed in the USA
BVOW001431240413

318988BV00007B/546/P